Parenting on Purpose:

RED YELLOW GREEN

FRAMEWORK

for Respectful Discipline

Ada Alden, Ed.D.

Crane Publishers
P.O. Box 41787
Plymouth, MN 55441

Parenting on Purpose:
A Red • Yellow • Green Framework for Respectful Discipline
By Ada Alden, Ed.D.

Published by Crane Publishers
Post Office Box 41787
Plymouth, MN 55441

Printed and bound in the United States of America

Cover and book design by Dan Lindahl

Edited by Judy Schell

Alden, Ada, Ed.D.
Parenting on purpose: a red • yellow • green framework for
respectful discipline/Ada Alden, Ed.D.
P. cm.
Includes sources and suggested readings.

Library of Congress Control Number: 2004102508

ISBN 0-9752599-0-3

1. Parenting 2. Discipline 3. Family relationships
4. Child growth and development
I. Title

649.6A358 2004

Acknowledgements

Writing this book has taught me many things. Of significance has been the sense of isolation that accompanies writing which is coupled with the critical need to have people who provide reassurance, emotional sustenance, prodding, and a willingness to share their talents. Writing this book has been by far my longest marathon. I am grateful to so many who have offered refreshing sips of water during the journey. The following are but a few who come to mind as the finish line nears.

I am indebted to the many parents who have communicated with me in so many ways that the messages within the book *Parenting on Purpose* had merit and were persuasive.

Dr. Jerry McCoy, a most amazing school superintendent said to me, "Ada, you should write a book." I have always found his remarks insightful.

I remember Mary Sheedy Kurcinka, a gifted author, stating clearly how important it was to have the book be in my voice.

Peggy Gilbertson, a skilled nurse practitioner, recognizes that good health care should include parent education. She included me in many South Lake Pediatric programs.

Bert Heaton listened thoughtfully as we ran through rain, snow and sleet.

Susannah Hill, now has children of her own, believed early on the insights made sense.

Kathy Weigelt is a parent educator in Early Childhood Family Education (ECFE) who loved the ideas and found them helpful in her classes.

Allan Vogt arrived with his daughter in an infant seat. She is now in elementary school and very connected to and with her father.

Jo and Charlie Keyes are now grandparents and have always encouraged me.

Barb Johnson, Renee Grassel and Martine Knothe were involved in the final editing, and loved the book. They assured me they felt honored to be asked. Their time was a gift.

Kathy Nomura clarified key points and assured me the ideas had merit. She is a smart parent who understood the challenge within the simplicity of the framework.

Arlene Bernardy took many classes, reviewed the book, and kept wondering when it would be done.

Lorraine Moore, Ph.D., carefully reviewed every page. She felt the book should be in every home. Her comments fueled me for another year.

Javan Larson, a wise teacher, encouraged the application of the Red • Yellow • Green Framework in other learning environments.

Jamie Eustace found the call numbers to assure librarians shelved my book correctly.

Linda Reinhardt and I run every Friday. She is a therapist and believes the book will be helpful in her practice.

Ellie Hyatt gently assured me that my efforts were noble, necessary, and worthy of publication. She believes the ideas on audio tape will enhance many a commute.

Judy Schell was a careful editor who encouraged me to write for the Eden Prairie Pay Day Post. She said I swam well when I finally got off the diving board.

Susan Hoch, a master librarian, always carried a flashlight to assist me in the dark and gloomy times. She has been a gentle sounding board and a thoughtful and thorough critical patriot.

Dan Lindahl is one of the most creative thinking artists I know. He understands pages needing air. He knows how to make my words comfortable in a brightly colored book.

Linda Lindahl's dining room table was a hospitable place for the writing team to work. She has been a trustworthy compass for years. I always call her when I'm lost and need direction.

My father, William E. Crane, taught me books were necessary and important teachers.

Victor and Virginia Alden were adoring and adored grandparents. They taught me about the importance of showing up and being present in the lives of those you love.

Cele and Duane Sours thought David and I were good parents. They provided hope, compassion, and adored us all. Duane is now 90 years old. He still assures me we are moving in the right direction.

My daughters, Heather and Elizabeth, are adults with families of their own. We share time, stories, and adventures. My daughters continue to be my most powerful teachers. I have always known being their mother was and is a privilege.

Although quite young, my grandchildren continue my education and have taught me about miracles.

My husband David has always believed in me and in us. Together we created the "Alden Way". Our dedication to one another jump-started parent conversations that led to the creation of the Red • Yellow • Green Framework. We needed and wanted to keep-talking, keep-believing, and keep-together. We still have family meetings.

For my mother Ella,
who died too soon.

Table of Contents

Chapter 6

Chapter 7

Chapter 8

Chapter 9

Chapter 10

Chapter 11

Chapter 12

Chapter 13

Chapter 14

Chapter 15

Chapter 16

Chapter 17

Preface

"I think the greatest source of courage is to realize that if we don't act, nothing will change for the better. Reality doesn't change itself. It needs us to act."

Margaret J. Wheatley - *Turning to One Another*

I have worked with parents for years. They have taught me many lessons. I know parents are powerful when it comes to what happens to their children. Parents do want what is best for their children, but are often poorly equipped to make smart decisions. With a few suggestions, I have seen parents make dramatic and long-lasting changes in their everyday lives. Parents need tools to provide structure and clarity. Parents need personal skill development as they relate to their ever-changing children. Parenting is difficult work. Parenting requires focus, intention and persistence. Parents are their children's most significant teachers. Lessons are taught, whether parents are responsive, demanding or neglectful. I know informed parents make better choices, choices which will help their children succeed not just in school but throughout life.

Too many parents are busy making decisions about their own adult futures. Many authors and entrepreneurs encourage parents to do just that: Live your lives and let others raise your children. Children want and need to be raised by their parents. Parents, however, are not sure how to do this. I wrote this book to assure parents they need to be purposeful about raising their children. I am not suggesting parents should become child focused; I am suggesting parents need to be child aware and child inclusive.

The concepts in this book allow adults to make choices that fit their own values. Our lives are complicated. We are very busy coming and going. The book's framework is flexible and simple. Some books I have read have been too hard to understand or too complicated to apply. In the heat of the moment, a parent can't run to a book and look up a solution. This book is about three colors. It asks, "Is this a Red? Green? or Yellow? moment." Parents can remember that.

My purpose in this book is to teach parents a way by which they can be intentional and reinforce the guidelines that matter in their lives. Children who live with predictable and consistent adults can spend their energies growing up. I have seen too many children who have been left to their own devices by caring, loving, albeit distant parents. Too many young children have been responsible for running their lives. I know that children who feel loved and secure thrive. I also know children need to have adults, particularly in the early years, who are in control, who set and enforce rules and limits. This book suggests a way to think about functioning with family members to assure home is a safe and respectful place for all. It is about when to say "yes" and when to say "no." It is also about knowing when the difference between "no" and "yes" is significant. The Red • Yellow • Green idea has room for psychological autonomy when children age.

Children need room to develop self-discovery and self-confidence, and to establish their own identity. This occurs over time. It requires parents being smart about kid life-issues and parent life-issues. My daughter said, "The Red • Yellow • Green Framework gives a method to deal with the madness."

This book is for intelligent, capable readers who want to develop their own skills and strategies for their own unknowns. There are no sure answers. This is not a prescription for success. Being an involved parent is not a once a month event. It is not reading a book-a-month. Available parents need to be just that – available.

When my children were young, I couldn't find a plan that worked for me. I created a plan that was flexible enough to age and move as we all aged and moved. The plan needed to work in changing situations. I needed to be smart with children of different ages, different temperaments and different dreams. I also needed a plan that helped my husband and me achieve our dreams.

Margaret Wheatley, a teacher and author, said, "It takes courage to start a conversation." Wheatley also believes that if we don't start talking to one another, nothing will change. I have written this book in hopes that the reader will eventually have important conversations with other adults about raising children. The book is meant to be a conversation, written as if the reader and I were talking. Sharing ideas and stories will help readers create their own Red • Yellow • Green Framework.

Introduction

Family Structure vs. Family Function

"The need for change bulldozed a road down the center of my mind."
Maya Angelou - I Know Why The Caged Bird Sings

The Red • Yellow • Green idea developed when I was struggling, scared and in need of help. I had taught first grade for years and was shocked when our first-born, Heather, was about 18 months old and I realized just how angry I could get at the child I adored, wanted and cherished. Actually, the sudden anger was personally as surprising as the rush of adoration and love I experienced when I first held her. Coupled with that rush was a clear, personal sense of ineptness and fear. I did not know how to care for her. I also knew she needed me to know. I needed to have a way of thinking about being a parent that would help when I was tired, confused and fearful. I realized I had much to learn and Heather would be a capable and willing teacher.

My mother died when I was 12 years old. I knew that a mother figure does have a significant presence in a child's life. I had no clear role model. I had no one to phone to ask for guidance. As a new mother, I had my wits and courage. I also had my loneliness and frustrations. I needed to make sense of it all, as Heather's future was dependent on her father and me making thoughtful smart choices.

Any model suggesting "this is the way to parent" is not a guaranteed strategy. No one really knows what is best for someone else. Parents are their children's most important early teachers. However, parents may be unaware of information about parenting that would be helpful and even necessary. In many conversations I have said, "Parents don't know what they don't know!" It is natural to parent as you were parented. But those carryover tactics may not achieve hoped-for relationships and connections. What was needed was something uncomplicated and easily remembered to implement when tempers flared or tired minds could not think.

This framework is a way to think about parenting. It is a simple, clear method to have a conversation about parenting strategies and techniques. I have even had conversations with myself, using this format as a way to organize my thoughts. If nothing else, the framework is a way to avoid doing harm. That alone is a significant step. I know of children who, as the result of destructive parenting, have considered themselves to be damaged goods.

We know the brain feeds off the environment. We know the brain's wiring is impacted by those first critical early years of interaction between a parent and his or her child. We know that poor parenting can permanently scar children. According to Dr. James Coleman, a sociologist, what happens in the home is twice as important as anything that occurs in the school in determining school success up to the age of 14. We know short-term, quick fixes do not meet long-term goals.

The Red • Yellow • Green Framework is a structure whose strategies provide parents a way to think about situations and make better choices in the home. The use of familiar colors is a way to promote individuals developing family connections, practicing family living skills, and establishing a sense of family unity. It is a strategy for family survival and celebration.

Designating strategies for parents using Red and Green creates a simple way to think and talk about the need for "no's" and "yes's" in a family's life. In this framework, Red designates the "no" and Green represents the "yes" for family expectations. Children can understand the use of color to help identify expected behaviors. Children can learn that "Hitting your brother is a Red Zone for us." "Wearing seat belts is a Green Zone for our family."

This framework is a simple communication tool. It is less threatening to say, "Let's clarify the Reds in our home," than it is to yell, "No one is in charge here. No one understands what we expect in this chaotic home." A childcare provider could extinguish a relationship with a parent by saying, "What kind of a parent are you?" However, the same childcare provider could initiate an important conversation by asking, "What are the Red and Green Zones in your home? What do you say 'yes' and 'no' to?" The Red • Green Zones are parent determined. They are the rules, limits and expected behaviors in the home.

The Yellow Zone is child-determined. A Yellow Zone could be a three-year-old deciding which shirt to wear. A Yellow Zone could be deciding what kind of cereal the child would eat for breakfast. A parent could say, "You choose the color you wish to have your room painted. That is part of the Yellow Zone in our family."

Careful consideration of the Red • Yellow • Green Framework will help parents make important decisions about children, calendars and everyday experiences.

Parenting is really about forging relationships and utilizing skills that establish connections which may last a lifetime.

The Red • Yellow • Green Framework evolved over a period of time. My children were key players in its construction. Their father and I worked hard to clarify our attitudes, align our behaviors and collaborate on strategies so that together we were about solution finding, not problem creating. The problems that emerged changed as our lives altered and our children grew from toddlers to inquisitive adolescents. We found it necessary to create new solutions on an on-going basis. We also learned quickly that effective solutions for Heather were not effective with our second daughter, Elizabeth.

My husband and I wanted to devise a parenting strategy which would allow a child's independence to flourish, but also have that child's sense of self-competency be couched within a consistent and predictable emotional awareness of being connected and belonging.

We wanted the "no" voiced by our children at age 2 to still be present at age 15. Adolescents are often confronted with situations where a "yes" assures a place in a group, but a "no" will remove them from drugs, alcohol and/or dangerous situations. This use of "no" is about independence of thought. A two-year-old "no" is often a defiant "no" to a parent's direction. It is a conflict with the two-year-old's hope for self-direction. Like everything else, saying "no" takes practice and learning. An adult "no" can and should be different from a child's "no." We wanted to equip our children with the "no" skills so important for their life journey. However, children cannot thrive in a too restricted "no" filled environment. Children deserve and need to experience opportunities that they initiate that are met with parental approval and a "yes" response. A clear understanding of what is acceptable and what is not promotes respect, a sharing of power, and a sense of being cared for and cared about for all household members.

To add to the complexity of "yes" and "no," it was important that David and I said "yes" and "no" to the same things. The trick is for both parents to know what they stand for, believe and value so "yes" and "no" are consistent along the way. In a one-parent household, worries about being in agreement are eliminated. In a one parent household, the parent still needs to take time to be sure actions and language are consistent with the parent's short and long-term goals. However, short and long-term goals do not need to match those of another adult in the household.

Parents want to do what is best for their child. Children want to grow up in a home with parents who are responsive and available psychologically and physically. Children need adult parents who are consistent, caring and capable. Children do not need parents who want to be the child's best friends.

I cannot tell you how to parent your child. I can only share this framework as a way to seriously consider your role as a parent and the powerful influence you have on your child. I know children learn what they live. Children are eminently aware of early teachers and their lessons. Parents are those early teachers and need to be intentional about the lessons they are teaching.

This framework is the result of nearly 30 years of thinking, implementing and revising. I believe the parenting journey is challenging, rewarding, exhausting, terrifying and grand. It is time to write about this journey because so many have requested that I do so. My children are young women now. I like them. They like me. This book is written with the hope that others will find my struggles, concerns and insights helpful. This book is written as a guide to assist parents as they seek their own answers and solutions. Each chapter ends with a short essay in hopes the stories will remain with the reader, after he or she has closed the book.

I started this book because my children have been such fine teachers. I worked on the book because my husband trusted in me and in us. I finished the book because my grandchildren are quite amazing. As I watch them, I realize my days, too, are flying by.

Reflection:

Mirror, Mirror on the Wall

According to Socrates, a life unexamined is not worth living. My children, since their early years, have held a mirror up to me. In this mirror I have been able to see my strengths, clarify my weaknesses and muster my courage.

Because of my children, I've discovered alternatives to the scream-shout-hit method of communication. I have learned that my actions are far more important than my eloquent speeches. I've risked sharing my fears with them and in turn have been reassured by their hugs. My children are not done with me yet. I do continue to examine my life and try to make it one of value. I wonder if Socrates was a parent?

Ada

Chapter 1

The Search for a Solution

"Your children are not your children. They are the sons and daughters of life's longing for itself."

Kahlil Gibran - The Prophet

I was a dedicated first grade teacher and could teach anyone to read. I was, like many new teachers, capable, enthusiastic and naive. I was effective in the classroom, and assumed those skills could easily transfer to the home when and if I had children of my own. How could raising a little one not be simple after skillfully maneuvering 24 six-year-olds for years?

I married and later we had a child. Heather didn't seem to be impressed with the fact that her mother had been a teacher. I was shocked to discover my inability to apply teaching skills to our everyday life. Heather was not interested in my plans. She was quite happy putting the farm animals in the schoolhouse. She was not interested in leaving the park when I thought it was a good time to depart. Rooms full of children used to respond to my requests with enthusiasm. Now I was unable to get my own child to bed or to come or to stop. What should I do with this child? How could I be there for her in a gentle and reassuring way? I also discovered that when I was tired, I was not the kind of parent I had hoped to be. I really did not get up in the morning intending to be a wretch. By 4:30 in the afternoon, my patience had waned. Sometime after Heather's nap and before dinner I realized I needed a plan.

During those early years, I remember thinking parenting was driving me crazy. Truth was, I was ill-equipped and skill-deficient. It was I, the mother, who needed to figure it out. I spent hours sitting at our kitchen table, feeling isolated and inept. It didn't appear to me that anyone else I observed was having trouble being a parent. My neighbors smiled a lot and their children appeared agreeable. I needed some way to look at the situation so that I could make smart and rational choices during difficult and stressful moments.

It didn't help matters that my husband and I weren't in agreement about the family rules and what children could do for themselves. Parenting differences were a challenge, but so were other aspects of how we viewed the way activities should be done. Actually, we each had a different idea about how to open gifts and how much tape was needed to wrap them. Jokes are made about squeezing toothpaste tubes, forgetting to put dirty clothes in the laundry basket, and leaving wet towels on the floor. All of these are important opportunities to practice talking about stuff. Discussing what appear to be small issues prepares couples for discussing the tough stuff. Unfolded socks, squished toothpaste and soggy towels can erode relationships over time. Ignoring issues by just tossing them into dark, out-of-sight corners just breeds mildew.

I went to a bookstore. Virginia Satir was a consultant, lecturer and author. Her emphasis is not on "sickness" but on the relationships between people that get in the way of positive communication. I liked her straightforward commentary. In *Peoplemaking*, she writes of the Family Map and interconnectedness – or lack thereof – between family members. Although separate individuals, family members are connected by a whole network of ties that impacts behaviors and tangles communication. Satir does a nice job of clarifying roles people play with simple drawings depicting each family member's head bedecked with the many hats he or she might wear. I was a wife, mother, teacher, friend, daughter and neighbor. Each role came with different behaviors and expectations. Interesting how a person can be screaming at a rambunctious four-year-old but when the phone rings, a quiet, reserved hello is possible. In a sense, a person wearing a different hat answered the phone.

David and I were clear about our "husband" and "wife" hats, as suggested by Virginia Satir. We needed some way to review, revise and design our "parent" hat. We were trying to figure out what being a mother and a father was. David liked to fish. I liked going to museums. But there was more to being a parent than fishing or picture looking. Being a parent was about protection, behavior reinforcement and behavior expectations. Establishing an agreed-upon parenting strategy was both a challenge and a requirement. Without some shared understanding, daily expectations were different, depending on who was in the room. Although we adored our children, we were inconsistent and confused. Having a child required discussions David and I had never had before.

Simple things were a struggle. What about nap time when people came to visit? What did we think made sense when it came to toy pick-up time? What were the expectations for mealtime? What things in the house should not be touched? Who put the puzzle pieces away and when? What was the response when child visitors jumped on furniture, threw apples in the street, or were reckless on the swing sets? What were we to do when both of our children wanted to sit next to the faucet in the bathtub?

These concerns may appear unimportant; however, I now know such questions are best addressed early. The family meeting, as described in chapter 15, is the perfect venue for these necessary talks. However, before family meetings can be efficient and effective, the adults need to practice, practice, practice. Family discussions get tougher and more necessary. Starting early is smart. Learning how to talk, disagree and clarify are life-long skills necessary for family living. Practice makes permanent.

The various roles family members play add to the confusion when it is necessary to communicate rules, routines, and expectations. Satir helped me understand that many times no one was listening to each other or actually even knew how to listen. She helped me understand how differently I reacted to situations as a wife or as a mother. When I visited my father, he only saw me as his daughter although my mother and wife roles were also present. David, my husband, was a son to his mother and a father to his daughters. As parents, David and I needed to be sure our parent hats were in agreement. David and I needed some way to be clear with one another as well as with our children. I knew we needed some way to provide clear and conscientious guidance while not squelching our children's enthusiasm and joy for life.

Confusion about how to parent added stress to the marriage. Being a loving wife and a caring mother often got in the way of each other. The world got complicated with pediatricians, baby sitters, grocery shopping and a lack of sleep. To add to the confusion, David was often traveling. I found that during the week, under my guidance and rule system, the family functioned pretty well. At least I was always right. When David came home on weekends, schedules, expectations and rituals were up for grabs. We had to figure out a way to provide consistent messages.

Techniques that were effective with a two-year-old didn't work when she was four. Lessons from the first child did not apply to our second. The mother hats are different, depicting how a mother reacts differently to different children. I used to sit up with the first child, checking to be sure she was breathing. With the second child, I celebrated when she was quiet. I did, however, notice our first child was so different from the second. My skills with Heather did not easily transfer to Elizabeth. Elizabeth moved quickly and asked questions later. Elizabeth was much more interested in her older sister, her older sister's stuff, and often found her mother in the way. Elizabeth understood on Monday that she was not to run in the street. That rule, however, might not have applied on Tuesday. She was always checking. Maybe the rule was different when it was raining?

Heather was quick to figure out that what her dad and her mother expected were different. She did what was expected depending on who was in the room. I knew that we needed a plan that encouraged personal competency, personal decision-making and a sense of personal discipline. What we needed was a way to talk about these issues without blaming, defending, or, worse yet, saying nothing. It needed to be flexible, as a rigid approach to child rearing left no room for individuality, change and maturation.

As a teacher, I understood different learning styles and appreciated individual differences. However, somehow we needed to promote a sense of us as a family. Everyone doing his or her own thing does not promote connection. We needed to come up with a clear, shared understanding of what and why some things needed to be done the same way. The "Alden Way" emerged. The "Alden Way" was the family rules and rituals. It was the way we, as a family, did things. The "Alden Way" was about "please" and "thank you." It was about sitting down and eating dinner together with the television off. The "Alden Way" was sharing chores, putting toys away and wearing seat belts. But, because Heather and Elizabeth were such different children, they needed to have their individual differences respected, nurtured and celebrated. Our daughters were unique and vibrant, not widgets to control. There needed to be room in the "Alden Way" for each of them to maintain her individuality and discover her own strengths and pathways. They each needed breathing room. It was our job as parents to figure out how to do that gently, consistently and responsibly. Assuring a pathway for each child does not mean "throw away the road maps."

The "Alden Way" was a guidance system and a suggested course upon which our children separately could travel in their own vehicles of their own design. However it was our job as parents to keep them out of ditches and avoid dead ends. I'm not suggesting the reader should follow the "Alden Way," but I do believe readers can come up with a Smith, Sanchez or Arnold Way. Come up with something that fits and works for you. I also think this needs to be purposefully done.

The framework explained in detail in the following pages is a pattern, a prototype, in which each family can place what makes sense and provides direction to achieve long-term dreams. I remember a parent who was so glad she stopped long enough to pay attention to how her family related to each other. She said without considering the relationships between each other she would have been remembered only for having clean toilets.

The Red • Yellow • Green Framework is easy to comprehend, but because child rearing is so complicated, application requires focus, persistence and determination. Through the years I have taught the model to hundreds of families. They have found it to be easily understood and, more important, easily implemented following adult conversations and zone clarification. Claiming new adult roles takes time, reflection and consideration. Children get in the way of careers, calendars and golf games. I believe that as a result of mindful discussions, mothers and fathers can develop a way of talking about their most challenging role of being their child's most important teacher. The conversation can begin when both partners understand and apply the simple parenting concepts within the Red • Yellow • Green Framework.

The plan can be done by one parent. Many successful single adults are raising caring and competent children. A family is made of those who live under one roof. Whatever the make-up or number, purposeful planning can promote connections and diminish a sense of isolation. Planning establishes the sense of "we are in this together."

The Red • Yellow • Green Framework is a way to think about discipline respectfully. *Discipline* **comes from the word** *disciple* **and is about teaching, not physical punishment.**

Children need a caring and consistent learning environment thoughtfully organized by caring and friendly adults in order to learn impulse control, language skills, respect, trust and manners. Parents who try to be their children's best friends often fail to be clear on limits, boundaries and the value of saying and meaning "no!" Children need parents who are friendly adults who provide guidance and consistency. Parents need to be able to say "I love you" and "I can't let you do that." A clear understanding and application of the Red • Yellow • Green model can help a parent create a consistent discipline framework from which thoughtful and well-planned decisions will emerge. It is a model that will impact both the parent and child and his or her individual sense of competency and being lovable.

Reflection:

Blankies, Bears and Other Necessities

Two-year-olds often drag their blankets into new experiences to help ease their fears. Often a blankie will provide comfort during times of stress. I know of an elderly gentleman who took his knitted afghan to the hospital to accompany him during surgery and recovery.

My husband has a very old used-to-be-red sweatshirt. When he has it on, it conveys an "at home," "relax," "all is OK" message. Through the years, the fire engine red color has faded and holes are easily visible. I have tried to discard it many times. It always returns to his closet, and like the Velveteen Rabbit, it works and is necessary.

We need to recognize the importance of special things in our life that help ease difficult transitions. Life is celebrated by those who have found a way to be comfortable with change and the unknown. Some carry blankies and bears. Others recognize the importance of afghans, old shirts and a way to think about disciplining respectfully.

I needed something simple to help get through the rough spots. I don't like tattered shirts. A primary color framework will have to do.

Ada

Chapter 2

Why a Framework of
Red • Yellow • Green?

"Messages received in childhood from parents, relatives, teachers, and friends are powerful influences on self-image."

Catherine Feste - The Physician Within

A parenting framework should be simple, clear and concise. It must be easily retrievable in moments of anger, exhaustion, frustration and glee. It cannot be so complicated that it sits on a shelf like the fancy candles Erma Bombeck talked about – candles that were never used because they were too good or too hard to find when you needed them. A framework using the primary colors Red, Yellow and Green with parents was recognized by most adults and provided a simple communication strategy. In pre-class questionnaires, parents associated Red with danger, stop and trouble. Comments about Yellow included "caution," "be careful" and "proceed carefully." Green made parents think of "go ahead" and "comfortable." What is helpful is that the colors seem to put parents at ease. They are worried enough about parenting and their children. The color concept is non-threatening, not a big cognitive leap and easy to remember. I think it gives parents a sense of hope that they can grasp the concept and it can prove to be helpful in family situations and relationships.

The Red • Yellow • Green framework is a way of thinking about a structure that helps build self-esteem and promote self-reliance in both parent and child. The plan provides a perspective for the future as well as survival skills for the present. It is grounded in the belief that relating respectfully is essential to long-term family relationships. This is a skill that can and should be learned.

The Red Zone is the "no" zone in which non-negotiable expectations are enforced. Reds are limits established by parents and caregivers. Reds are often based on the adult's responsibility to stop, protect and focus on safety first. Red Zone clarification by parents of young children is based on being an attentive and ever-watchful adult. As children age, however, the Red Zone is modified and is adapted to changing family expectations. Eventually the Red Zone becomes the "no" area for all family members. The Red Zone can be about no name-calling, no hitting, no taking things without asking or no using drugs. The Red Zone provides guidance and clarity about what is expected and respected. The Red Zone is the most challenging for the child and the easiest for the parent.

The Green Zone includes the "hurrahs" of everyday. It is the zone of recognition and acceptance. The Green Zone is the area of high fives and "well-done's." It is about noticing, smiling and emotional sustaining. The Green Zone is the "I love you" and "I like being with you" zone. The Green Zone is the "yes" message to a child which gives both guidance and reassurance.

Parents or caregivers are responsible for implementing the Red and Green Zones within the Red •

Yellow • Green Framework. This framework, when used effectively, provides a sense of emotional safety for the child.

The Yellow Zone is selected by the the child. The Yellow Zone in isolation creates a different dynamic which will be addressed in Chapter 6. If the Yellow Zone exists within the Red • Green Framework, the child-selected Yellow is parent observed. This zone promotes thinking skills and helps a child practice and learn self-reliance. This is the zone where parents or caregivers are available to develop, reinforce and support the child's initiative. When a child makes personal choices and decisions, the sharing of power promotes a feeling of trust among family members. The Yellow Zone is the most challenging for the parent. It includes sharing the power and appreciating the child's right to choose. The child feels trusted to make a good decision about which shirt to wear or which cereal to select. The parent learns he or she does not need to make all of the decisions. With this framework, adults and children have some power and a shared sense of respect, trust and connection.

A strength of the Red • Yellow • Green Framework is that the zones narrow or broaden to coincide with the individual child's development, skills and age. *(See the figure on page 72.)* It is vitally important that all zones function together. One zone alone does not meet the needs of the child. An all-Red Zone existence can be likened to being in a prison. A strictly Green experience, with every request earning a "yes" and all wishes granted, is about overindulgence and selfishness. A Yellow Zone in isolation depicts a lonely, disconnected, unattached existence.

The Yellow Zone standing alone is like living day to day without anyone giving you a valentine. Essential to the framework's success is the relationship and interconnectedness between all three zones. Any zone in isolation could prove not only ineffective but harmful.

The Red • Yellow • Green Framework offers an approach based on the belief that the child is to be included in the family. The three zones functioning together teach belonging, a feeling of "us," and, more importantly, help define family members as a unit. The framework will sustain the adults and the children involved as they develop a relationship and practice life skills necessary to navigate the months and years ahead.

Parents need to understand each zone separately before they can construct a model that fits their own needs, wants, hopes and dreams. This model fits across all cultures. However, adults need to determine the specific form it will take.

The framework establishes early the importance of being purposeful about the family. Early implementation of the Red • Yellow • Green Framework will hopefully avoid later need for family repair. I think of the Red • Yellow • Green concept as a way to plan ahead and to chart a direction. A long distance runner knows that drinking water when he or she is really thirsty is too late. Before running it is necessary to drink water and prepare. A construction worker carefully lays the foundation before putting up the walls and roof. Going on a canoe trip requires careful route selection, meal planning and equipment organization. Taking a lengthy trip without careful planning is not only foolish but possibly dangerous. The runner, the construction worker and the canoeist all know about early planning. Parents, too, would profit from early preparation and purposeful skill development.

This framework is not something to try when family members have lost touch with each other and are living boarding house lives. This is not a tool for families who find themselves in terrible conflict and emotional crisis. Families who are too frantic will not be able to slow down long enough to have the thoughtful conversations necessary to create a Red • Yellow • Green Framework. In these instances, professional and supportive help is required. To continue the metaphor, using this model is not a good idea when family members are struggling in a canoe, searching for a campsite without food, fuel or protection. This is for those who are preparing for the journey.

To assure understanding and implementation, I will discuss each of the zones of the framework separately. Discussion of how the zones need to be interconnected includes examples and strategies for adults who are considering the application of the framework. The suggestions, however, are intended only to jump start necessary conversation so that the framework fits the chart of the journey each family selects. This book does not dictate the destination or the direction. However, it offers a good way to think about how to pack, plan and prepare. Hanging the bookmark, which comes with this book, on the refrigerator will act as a helpful prompt.

A father encouraged me to include this bookmark so that he would not forget the important questions to consider before acting. "Is this a Red Zone?" "Should I remember to reinforce my child by commenting on positive behaviors as encouraged in the Green Zone?" "Is this a Yellow Zone?" "Is this something I should quietly observe?" "Is this action my child's choice?" The colors on the refrigerator act as a tickler file, a friendly reminder of the framework.

Reflection:

Parenting Potholes

Parenting is an incredibly difficult occupation. The job description continues to astound me. Actually, I reviewed my "parent expectation and duty sheet" recently, and I'm not sure I'm up to the task. I do know that periodically I have trouble with the potholes that occur in parenting. These abnormalities in the road seem to throw our faulty communication system into havoc. It's tough living together. I believe in clean rooms, picked up toys, pleasant conversation and consideration of others. These cheery hopes are not always a reality. When mired in a rut, I try to regroup, to find quiet moments, to rediscover within me the quiet courage, resolve and commitment required to be a parent.

I believe in children solving problems, raising questions, verbalizing their anger, sharing their feelings and being responsible. Our children have not been directed to go to their rooms and come out smiling. They know they can safely disagree with us. They know loving one another does not require agreeing with one another. An emotional safety is present when children know parents will be there "no matter what." Children can verbalize their anger, their disappointments, and clearly articulate their ever-changing needs. I remember telling Heather, "I don't know how to be the mother of a four-year-old." She looked at me with a shocked and disappointed eye. "Well, I don't know how to be four either!" she snapped.

Years have passed. I still find this job a challenge. I wonder as I sit in a pothole if I'm on the wrong road. However, I keep listening, keep believing and keep trying to live in a home where we are not afraid of intimacy and are suspicious of silence. I don't want to live in a boarding house. A father once told me his children no longer argued and were now quiet. Every room came equipped with a television. Intimacy, connection and a sense of belonging are not nurtured in a "too-quiet, everyone do your own thing" household. I want us all to be able to share joy, triumphs, dead ends, and achievements. I don't want our lives to be ones of pre-approved fluff.

Alan Alda talked about being brave enough to live "life creatively." Parenting requires bravery, creativity, endurance and persistence. We must recognize that change, risk, and life offer no simple answers. Having a child immediately moves an adult from a sense of comfort into a parent "wilderness of intuition." Family living requires hard work and many times not knowing what to do. Indeed, it is an adventure not available on a long distance jet flight. The journey includes moments in potholes faced with our own humanness and foibles. But there are also open stretches when the journey is smashing.

I'm in for the long ride. I know there will be speed bumps, detours and some cruising. I know about road construction and delays. However, when I look at my daughters, I am in good company.

Ada

Chapter 3

The Red Zone:
The Non-Negotiables

"Think not those faithful who praise all thy words and actions, but those who kindly reprove thy faults."   *Socrates*

The Red Zone in the framework is necessary and needs to be gently present. It consists of the "no's" in a child's life. Actually, the Red Zone is life-saving for young children. The Red Zone includes electric outlets, stairs, stray dogs, strangers, swimming pools and children unattended in cars. The Red Zone needs consistent monitoring.

This zone changes based on the age of the child. *(See the figure on page 72.)* Parents need to be diligent about child safety, particularly in the early years. That is the Red Zone. The car does not move unless everyone is wearing a seat belt. The Red is the "No! I can't let you do that." It defines that which is not accepted in the family. The Red Zone must be clear. Positive guidance comes from maintaining the Red Zones of no hitting, no name-calling, no taking other people's stuff without asking. Other important behavior lessons might include no running through the fast food restaurant pushing the spigots of soft drink machines or no ball throwing in the house. Purposeful observation and maintenance of the Red Zone instruct children on how to behave.

By carefully maintaining the Red Zone, parents assure that the life lesson of respecting one another is taught. Certainly Red Zones for babies and toddlers would not apply to all in the family. Babies will fall down the stairs until they learn how to maneuver them. Children may not be near water until they learn how to swim. Children cannot run around in a store parking lot without holding an adult hand. Once a child learns to climb stairs, swim and walk with an awareness of moving cars, these Red Zones become part of the child's internal guidance system. The Red Zone does, however, become more complicated as children age. When children get older, they become part of a Red Zone that applies to all family members.

Initially, the early Red Zone is about safety and is easily implemented by parents. Being consistent with Red Zone expectations requires a clear, consistent and persistent message. Some confusion results when the adults caring for a child have different Red Zones. If dad says no playing in the closet, and mom thinks closet playing is ok, the child learns different ways to behave based on who is in the room. When dad is present, stay out of the closet. When mom is in the room, the closet is available to explore. Eating dinner in the living room might be acceptable to one parent and unacceptable to another. Although these are seemingly innocuous situations, they offer the opportunity for discussion, clarification and agreement on what and how we will live with one another.

Parents and caregivers need to take time to agree on what is not acceptable in the home. A consistent message teaches what is acceptable and what is not.

When our daughters were young, neighbors came over to play. The children bounced on the sofas, leapt from the chairs and considered our living room to be a workout room. Both Heather and Elizabeth were wide-eyed. I informed the visitors that furniture leaping behavior was not acceptable at our house. I told the visiting children they could stay, but not leap on the furniture. I ignored their parents' comments on developing gymnastic skills. The Red Zone needs to be clear even when visitors come. It wasn't acceptable for anyone to be jumping on the couch. If Heather and Elizabeth saw children jumping on the couch, they would have learned that guests can do what they could not. Another possible lesson was that guests could do what they wanted, and eventually that could lead to problems when friends come to visit during high school years and beyond. As children get older, parents need and want their children to maintain family rules when friends come to visit.

William, age five, came to play quite often. He liked to spit in the yard. I told him spitting was not acceptable at our house. He mentioned how his father spit. I encouraged him to go home and spit with his father. However, at our house spitting was not a community activity. I think I said something about after you brush your teeth, spitting is recommended. William came throughout the summer, but never spit again at our house. I have no idea what went on at his home. My daughters are still not public spitters.

Early messages about how we live and sit on the furniture provide a wonderful opportunity to begin necessary conversations that will be revisited for years to come. When our children were teenagers, friends came to visit and the family rules were maintained. Friends came for parties, but no alcohol was served and movies were not "R" rated. Parents have often shared stories about what happened in their homes when their children's friends brought beer and sexy films to a get-together. The excuse was "My friends brought it. What was I to do?" Saying "no" teaches "no." It also is an opportunity for children to say, "We can't have that here. My parents don't allow that."

Throwing food on the floor, not clearing the table after eating, leaving toys strewn throughout the house, running around a restaurant, rearranging videos at the video rental store, throwing trash on the street, mashing greeting cards on racks and using verbally abusive language all were opportunities for teachable moments focused in and on the Red Zone.

The Red Zone reassures the child that there are limits. Loving your child includes saying "no." The Red Zone helps a child acquire skills necessary for civil community living and respectful family relationships.

The non-negotiables of the family are housed in the Red Zone. The Red Zone needs to be clear to all in the family. This Zone helps children develop a sense of security by providing some predictable guidelines.

As our children got older, leaving the house without sharing destinations landed in the Red Zone. As family members, we needed to know where each of us was. Each of us shared our whereabouts. It was a way of connecting and caring. As our children aged, they continued to let us know where they were going. It was the way we did things. I let everyone know when I was shopping and when I would be home. We knew when people were bowling, going to a movie or staying with a friend. One evening, David and I went to dinner and got home unusually late. The music was good and we listened. We came home to very disgruntled daughters. They commented that we were late and hadn't called. They were concerned. They also pointed out that "that wasn't the way our family did things." They were right, of course. We had been negligent. It is also important to note that both David and I were comfortable with the girls pointing out the error of our ways. Our coming home late without calling was a Red Zone concern. That comes with the Red • Yellow • Green Framework. Parents are held accountable as well as children.

Parents should not only worry about their children not listening to them. Parents need to worry also about their children watching them.

Parents are powerful in the eyes of their children. Parents have the ability to notice, ignore, accept or reject. I have watched little ones quake when a parent catches them taking a cracker from a bowl. I have seen fear in the eyes of a young child when parents yell. I also have noticed the relief and immediate sense of calm when a crying child is eased in the arms of his or her mother. Children yearn to be cared for and about by their parents. Even children who have been abused or neglected have cried themselves to sleep because they so miss their parents.

Adults with whom I have worked tear up when they speak of their parents. I have never attended a funeral for a parent when the children did not cry. They either weep for the parent they had or the parent they wish they had had. Parents are powerful. How they use that power can have a life-long impact on the child. The Red Zone is about using this power respectfully with long-term ramifications in mind.

The Red Zone is part of the important connection between all three zones. A Red Zone ONLY would be abusive and would damage a child's spirit and soul. To be told always "no," "not now," or "you can't" sucks the life energy from a child's spirit. A child cannot learn on an empty spirit. A child brought up in only a "no" zone will eventually fail to thrive, and will grow up damaged. The next chapters detail Green and Yellow Zones which balance, counteract and interconnect with the Red Zone.

Reflection:

Hazards of Growing Up Alone

Trouble has been averted. Quick action by Mike Wallace, the leader of the California Condor Recovery team, has probably saved the species. Condors were nearly extinct. In 1982 only 22 birds were left. They are impressive large birds that fly along the California coast. Condors have a 10-foot wingspan and are one of the world's largest flying birds. To save the birds, dramatic steps were taken.

In the late '80s, birds were captured and did reproduce successfully. But the whole project fell apart when the newly hatched birds could not reenter the wild due to their bad behavior. In 1992, hopeful, hard working condor breeders were dismayed to discover the captive raised birds were naughty.

On certain windy days the birds would fly to the Pine Mountain Club and watch people barbecuing. Other days they would circle the parking lot and vandalize the building, destroy windshield wipers and damage equipment. Mike Wallace described their behavior as something right out of Lord of the Flies. *That book is about boys living on an island, running wild. No structure, no limits and no guidelines were in place. Members of the Pine Mountain club were not condor fans and helped maintain the 30 to 40 percent mortality rate of the condor marauders.*

The "save the condor" group devised a new plan. It turns out condors are like primates and need to learn how to behave from

37

their parents. After hatching, condor chicks were cared for by humans wearing a condor hand puppet. During the feeding, chicks were able to observe adult condors and learn appropriate condor etiquette.

In the wild, condors are raised in a secluded nest with two stern and hierarchical parents. Chicks are not allowed to roam, fly wild or act inappropriately. Careful condor parenting includes high expectations and clear condor house or nest rules. When the birds were older, they were sent into the wild with a mentor bird. The "save the condor" group eventually raised well behaved birds who did not vandalize the Pine Mountain Club.

Parents who provide no limits, who are unavailable emotionally or physically, or who do not hold children accountable, promote bullying behavior. It seems that both children and condors need adults who are available, consistent and persistent. It seems neither chicks nor children can grow up alone. If they do, we all are eventually victims.

Ada

Chapter 4

The Green Zone:
Approval and Celebration

"When you love someone, you love him as he is"   *Charles Péguy*

"Each child from infancy needs to be told with words and actions that she is lovable and important. Parents must accept this responsibility."
Madelyn Swift - Discipline for Life: Getting It Right With Children

The Green Zone in the framework is the area that is celebrated. It is the behavior that is approved, encouraged, valued and reinforced. The Green Zone is the good job, hurrah for you, and, eventually a hurrah for me area. Young children thrive on being told that what they are doing is acceptable, encouraged or appreciated. I have watched a two-year-old say with clarity and pleasure, "I did it!" A 16-year-old shared how delighted she was with herself after she had worked out at the YMCA. When children are young, it is the adults in their life who provide support and education about what is a Green Zone hurrah and what isn't. Paying attention to the Green Zone early in life will result in children learning about and experiencing approval, behavior selection and positive behavior reinforcement.

Ray McGee, a psychologist and teacher, talked extensively about "catching them being good." Using the Green Zone is often hard for parents. It seems when children are behaving well, parents tend to be quiet. They don't want to disturb the pleasant scene. However, hearing positive comments, catching an approving smile, or sensing parental approval reassures the child and reinforces to the child the idea that he or she is on the right track. "Good job!" "I like being your mom." "It is wonderful when you and I sit here together and eat breakfast." "I find you to be good company." "I like reading books with you." "I noticed you found the cereal box that matched the coupon." "Thanks for helping with the dishes." These are all Green Zone reinforcing comments.

As children age, the behaviors receiving Green Zone assurance change, but the need to be noticed doesn't. Children like parents showing up for soccer games, plays, school events and scout meetings. A parent shared how she always goes to concerts at the middle school. Many children are just dropped off at the door. Parental appearances, applause and smiles are longed for, even though middle school children appear disinterested. Celebrating birthdays, finding money from the tooth fairy and going on walks together promote a sense of being valued.

At our house, holiday celebrations are important. Stories every night before bedtime teach "you are important to me." Although reading aloud is important for language learning and appreciation, reading aloud also teaches that the parent has purposefully taken time to share moments together. Spending time together matters. Driving children to and from the dentist and French horn lessons, and assisting in the cookie drive are all evidence that the Green Zone is present and viable.

However, using the Green Zone alone can also be a form of overindulgence as researched by Jean Illsley Clarke. Many children who have been given all of the stuff in life have not been included in the family work. Children who are always reassured, reinforced and allowed to run free eventually ache for authentic relationships and an appreciation of genuine ability and accomplishment. A stand alone Green Zone is evidence of a lack of responsible behavior on the part of the parent and creates a relationship that is without structure and boundaries. Too much Green Zone is like over-watering plants. They eventually drown and die. Children who are only reassured, only complimented and only given kind comments are children who assume their way is the only way. According to Madelyn Swift, "Too often overindulgence of children leads to a family which is child-driven. Families need to be parent-driven."

A Green Zone-heavy environment is like eating too many Thanksgiving dinners. Parents who are Green Zone heavy are avoiding limit-setting and saying "no." This zone in the model is about attentive parenting, not over-permitting or overindulging. Some parents become mesmerized by the wonder of their child. They gush and reinforce every burp, goal or accomplishment, large and small. The Green-saturated child eventually will have tough life lessons ahead. A stand alone Green Zone is a form of negligence. The future can be very difficult for children when parents mistakenly make it too easy for children in the present.

The Green Zone requires daily tending and awareness. The challenge, of course, is for parents to agree on what is allowed and what is unacceptable in the home. What are the behaviors we will reinforce? If parents don't agree on the Green Zone, children will get different messages depending on who is present. Mom expects me to put the dishes away. Dad doesn't comment if the table is not cleared. One parent may be delighted with a young child leaping on a table. The other parent may find table climbing unacceptable. Consistency and persistence need to be present when the Red and Green Zone are interconnected. Actually, a single parent in the home eases possible confusion if that parent maintains consistent messages.

The Green Zone provides ample opportunity to nurture the child's growth and assure direction. The Red Zone balances and clarifies the dynamics of the growth and life force of the Green Zone. Children need boundaries in order to feel safe. Growing up takes energy and effort. Children need coaching and guidance. Purposeful parenting is not just being a cheerleader. Being aware of the right behaviors, providing hugs and saying "I love you" consistently requires dedication over time.

Reflection:

Miracles Aren't Tough

The woman came up to me after a seminar on parenting. She had sat quietly during the presentation, nodding periodically. Ninety minutes later, she stood quietly near my papers while I answered questions.

"I need to tell you about the miracle at our house," she said.

She had heard me speak a year ago about sharing affection and letting each other know you care. I had told the story of Elizabeth who had assured us she was growing up in a perfect family. I was delighted to hear that. The reason, Elizabeth said, had nothing to do with my being a parent educator. Elizabeth said that what really mattered was how, whenever she left the house, someone said, "Good-bye Elizabeth. I love you." Elizabeth was in third grade and perfect was easily defined.

A year ago, the woman went home and told her husband the importance of saying "I love you." He shrugged and suggested that the kids already knew. She persisted. "They have to be told. They need to hear the words." With tenacity, she struggled on. Finally, they began telling their children, the oldest a senior in high school, that they were loved.

Initially the kids looked away. Initially no one acted differently. Initially there was a continued quiet. As weeks passed, the hugging, the laughter, the departures included "I love you."

The miracle happened when her daughter went to the University of Minnesota in Duluth. She called her mother and said, "I love you, mom. I miss hearing you and dad say you love me." The woman thanked me. "You changed our lives."

Many miracles occur in the home. During the holidays, I will measure success by the number of cloth napkins I'll have to iron. I will know we had lovely conversations because my candle supply will have to be replenished. Table napkins and used up candles are evidence of shared table conversations. I will be thankful for times together. I will celebrate the shared discussions, opportunities to pass the potatoes, and to bow our heads in gratitude around the candlelit table. I will be sure that those I love will know they are dear to me. Such messages are like warm cloaks that provide protection from chilly winds and dropping temperatures. "I love you" messages are miracles. When you are 90, you will never regret saying "I love you." Actually, saying it is a way to celebrate what is right with the world.

Ada

Chapter 5

Red • Green Zones:
Rules, Rituals and Routines

"Our children are counting on us to provide consistency and structure. Children need parents who say what they mean, mean what they say, and do what they said they were going to do. These parents provide a basic backbone structure for children to function."

Barbara Coloroso - Kids Are Worth It!

"To lose patience is to lose the battle."   *Mahatma Gandhi*

Although three colors create the recommended framework, it is helpful to understand how the Red and Green operating together can be effective, albeit for a short time. For long-term success, the Yellow Zone needs to be present. However, early on, parents can be successful by placing all of their energies into careful Red and Green Zone construction.

It's important to consider the Red and Green Zones together. Thoughtful consideration of the "yes" (Green Zone) and "no" (Red Zone) establishes an environment that teaches the child someone else is watching out for and with him or her. The two zones act like emotional boundaries that promote security and a sense of safety. The Red Zone acts with the Green Zone in a check and balance manner. Children are growing up the best way they know how. They need parents who reassure, reinforce and encourage as well as stop, prevent and monitor. These Zones are parent-determined. The Red Zone is the "No, I can't let you do that." The Green Zone is the "Yes! Well done. I see you are getting it," domain. They provide the framework for the core values of respect, trust and care. Together the Red and Green Zones comprise the limits and/or rules and the behavior that is accepted and cultivated in the family. Together they define the family "way" of doing things.

Children raised in homes where the Red and Green are clear, consistent and parent-determined, grow up knowing what their parents consider right and wrong and how to follow parent guidelines. This framework does help parents raise dutiful children, up to a point. Dr. David Walsh, noted national speaker on the impact of the media, says parents who are not teaching their children right and wrong are allowing other teachers to define what is or is not acceptable. Walsh speaks eloquently about television and video games and their lessons of violence, disregard and vulgarity.

During the adolescent years, I have observed some children flounder – children who were raised in homes with too rigid parent-determined Red and Green Zones. When parents make all of the decisions, children don't learn how to decide, to choose or to plan a course of action. When children are in the adolescent years, they are learning how to be adults. They grapple with dependence and independence. Children may take one of two paths, neither of which achieves the long-term outcomes of self-discipline and competence. One path is to turn against the established Red and Green and claim independence. The other option is to find someone else to provide the Green and Red guidance as the child has not developed a personal decision-making ability. All decisions have been made for him or her by caring but overcontrolling parents.

A parent wanted his son to be an Eagle Scout. The father, active as a scoutmaster, was busy planning trips, completing papers and selecting projects. The father became so enamored with the idea of his son becoming an Eagle Scout that his "ideal son" became the driver. The ideal son vision clouded his view of the son he had. The message was "my son will be an Eagle Scout." One badge before completing the requirements, the boy dropped out. He utilized his independence and decided his father couldn't make him complete the requirements. After four years at a university, he quit one credit shy of graduating. Although his parents had reinforced the "yes" (Green Zone) and "no" (Red Zone), he rebelled. It is possible he would have completed the scout work and the university graduation had they not been such critical outcomes of success for his father. Somewhere in the growing up years, the message became "my Eagle Scout, college graduate son," rather than "my son is enough who and how he is."

The adolescent's job description includes becoming his or her own person. This son sought independence and found his direction, based not on an inner compass but on an externally-applied expectation and what appeared to be a mandate from his parents. By his behavior, the son appeared to state, "You can't make me." His parents didn't and couldn't.

The Red and Green Zones are parent-selected, parent-reinforced and parent-monitored. Rules are clear and what is valued is clear as well. Up to the time of early adolescence, results are immediate and positive. With only a Red and Green present, the family "way" to do things is understood; however, it does not hold as children mature and move into young adulthood. As a child matures, he or she needs space in which to make some decisions. The child needs to practice decision-making and problem-solving. As a child reaches the adolescent years, developmentally his or her task is to move toward independence. The child will have many opportunities to make personal choices and personal decisions. The Yellow Zone option becomes quite prominent during the adolescent and young adult years. A parent-determined and reinforced Red • Green Zone without a Yellow Zone results in a child who is unable to make personal choices. A too-late arriving Yellow Zone is evidenced by a child who has had insufficient practice in making choices and learning to think ahead before selecting an option or action.

Another outcome of a Red and Green only model is a child who is seeking others to make decisions for him or her because he or she is unsure about making choices having had no practice doing so. For example, a young woman who went to the East Coast met a religious leader who assured her he knew the right and wrong choices necessary for life. He, in fact, knew the Red and Green Zone options. The young adult daughter promptly gave the man her inheritance of millions of dollars. She needed someone else to show her the way. The potential hazard of a Red and Green only framework may be either a rebelling or a following young adult.

I met a young man who is an ethicist and full professor. Most of all, his parents wanted a Ph.D. son. The parental Red and Green were created with a Ph.D. son outcome in mind. During his first year of college he was told not to come home at Thanksgiving if he still was pulling his hair back with a rubber band. When I met him, he had quite an impressive ponytail, had been teaching with a Ph.D. for years, and had never been home since his first year of college.

Too much Red and Green may apply too much pressure on a child's life. Each child, somewhere along the way, needs to have the opportunity to find his or her own way. Gibran, in *The Prophet,* talks about parents as the bow and children as arrows. Too much controlling of the arrow may end with the child only trying to get away – not towards something.

Children raised with only clear Reds and Greens are vulnerable to peer pressure or outside influences as they age. These children have been raised with an ear for external directions and external expectations. Eventually, they will seek outsiders to provide guidance and direction, since through the years they never practiced making personal decisions or solving problems. The opportunities to practice self-competency and self-responsibility were lost.

The Red and Green alone leave no room for the child to grow individually or to self-actualize. Red and Green, though necessary, are not enough. Young people are at risk when they don't have the opportunity to practice personal skills and always seek others to be the guide. When everything is decided, planned and orchestrated, the child never learns about consequences, long-term planning and regrouping when plans fail. When the Red and Green Zones are all there is, the message can become "My parents made me do it." "They act like I can't do anything without them telling me what to do."

Remember what powerful communicators parents can be. "You can't do it" messages seep into a child's inner sense of self and eat away personal confidence.

A parent always did all of the packing for her children to be sure they had the right stuff for a weekend or week-long trip. She didn't want them to be ill prepared. I remember when our five-year-old Elizabeth packed for a weekend away and only brought her stuffed animals. In the motel, she realized that a nightgown and toothbrush might have been helpful. She learned the consequence and took responsibility. Through the years, she learned how to pack. She developed the skill over time. She always packs for herself and no longer limits her choices to elephants and bears.

A sixth grade boy on his way to overnight camp was angry at his mother because she had not packed correctly. His parents had taught him packing was the mother's job. His job was to be sure she did it right. Child packing and camp preparation skills were never developed. However, the child did learn to blame others when things weren't right.

The implementation of the Red • Green Zone is useful when raising very young children. Parents of young children are clear about what is and isn't acceptable. Parents make choices; children respond. Children learn what is right and wrong and how to manage in an environment that has been prescribed. This parent determination of what is acceptable and what isn't takes time, energy and persistence. Children raised in a household clear about Red and Green feel loved and know adults are there for them. What they don't know is whether they are there for themselves. Parents hold all of the power. Parents need to share the power in order to promote a sense of self-confidence, personal problem-solving and personal competency. As the child ages, these skills are important if he or she is going to make positive choices in the adolescent years. In a Red and Green home without a Yellow Zone, children learn to follow. However, when they are always following, they are not practicing leadership or self-care decisions.

To prepare a child to make wise choices, a golden time to provide opportunities for this skill development exists between the ages of two and 15. Certainly young children learn self-help skills and can accomplish learning many important life-long skills. However, elementary years herald a parenting opportunity. In order to use this opportunity, however, a parental shift is required. Parents need to observe while the child makes choices. The child needs to practice trying things out within the safety of the home. When Elizabeth packed her stuffed animals, it was a short trip and her parents were near to provide assistance. Elizabeth started learning this important skill at five years.

Making their own choices gives children the opportunity to experience the consequences of their actions. Children learn how to do things right and take responsibility for that. Personal choice and personal action teach "I can do it." Giving an allowance to a five-year-old allows the child time to learn money management. By the time the child is 15, he or she will have 10 years of opportunity to practice making change, saving, losing and loaning. The opportunity to practice, learn and discover individual skills is the property of the Yellow Zone.

It is during the adolescent years, when seeking autonomy and understanding self is the child's task, that a narrow "do it the parent way" approach may lead to difficulties and, more importantly, a child who is not prepared to make smart and wise choices.

The lesson learned in a Red • Green-only environment is "I can do it" only when the parent points the way and arranges the experience. The parent is the decision-maker and is responsible for the outcome. Actually the parent gets to be responsible for the good, bad and the ugly.

Reflection:

Grandmother's Clock

We own a grandmother clock made in 1825. She is lovely. The face is hand-painted and the wood is a lovely rich, dark brown. It must be wound each day. It has no plug, no battery, no solar energy box. Someone, usually me, must give it attention daily or it stops.

Too often our goal is to acquire things that make our lives easier or require little attention. We also can hire someone else to do a job. Flyers encourage us to have someone else mow, wash windows and paint. The sales pitch usually includes something about the task taking too long and getting in the way of our lives. Fast food restaurants wave coupons and banners suggesting they will cook for us. The message implies that cooking your own meals takes too much time. The message between the lines is to have someone else do it. Beware of such beguiling ads.

My children are like my clock. Each day they need attention. Each day they need me to reassure, to rewind and to admire gently. No child can learn on an empty spirit. Each day I fill my child up and give her a sense of connection. I know it is my job and not one to be outsourced.

Battery run clocks do not emit quiet, reassuring, ticking sounds. Isolated children do not give unsolicited hugs. Parenting is for everyday. It takes time and no one else can do it.

Ada

Chapter 6

The Yellow Zone:
Do Your Own Thing

The Monster

"You're afraid of me. I throw things. I hit people. You pretend not to see. I talk back and you do nothing. You never tell me what I should or shouldn't do. You're afraid of me. And I'm scared. Who knows what you might let me do? Please. Please tell me where to stop. Don't be afraid of me."

Author unknown

"Children who have conquered problems build the belief system: I can think for myself and I can solve problems."

Madelyn Swift – Discipline for Life: Getting It Right With Children

The Yellow Zone is child-determined; the Red and Green are adult-decided. In the Yellow Zone the child has choice, option and power. If the Yellow Zone is too wide, too soon, the child may develop a life-attitude that is without rules, boundaries or relationships. Dorothy Briggs in *Your Child's Self Esteem* reminds us that children also need a sense of self-competency. This can be nurtured and encouraged in the Yellow Zone. However, using the Yellow Zone alone is like using the Red and Green Zones alone and is potentially damaging. When used appropriately, the Yellow Zone provides children with the opportunity for exploration and self-expression. When it exists alone, it is about isolation and disconnection and some consider it a form of emotional neglect. Growing up unattended or feeling disconnected without an adult taking the time to say "yes" or "no" is the nightmare of the Yellow Zone. Children who make all of their own choices, cook all of their meals, and survive often on grit, are perhaps competent, but they develop without relationships that reassure, value and unconditionally accept.

I got the idea of the Yellow Zone when I observed parents and children living together but avoiding interacting with one another. Bill Moyers, a noted journalist, has written about children who are being raised by appliances. These seem to me to be Yellow Zone-only children.

When our children were young, neighborhood children used to come over to our house in the early evening. They were bright, interested and liked playing with books and puzzles. They delighted in coming over to play and often asked to stay for dinner. I always asked them to call their parents for permission, but they assured me their parents would not care. Calling home before they stayed for dinner was my requirement. These are the children who rode their tricycles down the middle of the street and were never hit. These children were the ones who would trick or treat late into the night. They were the children our daughters considered quite lucky to live such free lives. Those lucky children always got to watch more television, have more allowance and enjoy more fun. As these children grew, they were often at the junior high and high school events seeking a ride home. They managed to make decisions and choices to get through their day. Many made good choices, but many also longed for someone who would care where and who they were.

These Yellow Zone children grew up without parent interference or support. These children were often bright and exuded confidence and a sense they didn't need anyone. I wondered if these children might not ache for someone to want them to be an Eagle Scout. They might have liked someone caring whether or not they ate dinner at a neighbor's home. Many of these kids had lots of toys, clothes and trendy items, but seemed to be emotionally empty.

I remember a child who appeared to me to have a Yellow Zone existence commenting on how lucky Elizabeth was to get hugs in the morning. Her parents were always too busy. I remember how she stayed inside our house, waiting for the school bus. I would hug Elizabeth before she left. Sometimes her friend got a hug from me too. I would ask first, and I still recall the shy smile and her saying, "That would be nice. I don't get hugs at home."

I taught a class of high school seniors and was surprised to find out how many of them had televisions in their bedrooms. A high percentage of the students ate dinner with a television as a companion. At the end of class, a young woman said she always ate alone. Her mother brought her dinner to her room and then returned downstairs to eat with her father. She wished they would invite her to join them. It is possible the parents thought that private eating was what the child wanted. I will always remember her dismayed look and how she shared this with me. I suggested she tell her mother that she would like to join them.

Sometimes what we think children may want may, in fact, not be the case. Parenting is not a job with easy answers and quick solutions.

Ongoing and consistent conversations are necessary to be sure the Red • Yellow • Green Zones which compose the framework are understood and clear.

In my experience, these children were taken care of but not cared for. They appeared to move into adulthood feeling lonely. I am not sure they felt loved. They took care of themselves but did not have parents who stayed up waiting for them to get home. No one yelled when they were late, wanted the car too often or failed to clean up their rooms. They didn't know about parents who expected certain behaviors, attendance at family events, or proper completion of tasks at home. Eating at the dinner table and learning good table manners were not expected. They didn't have to write thank you notes, vacuum, or share in the dog responsibilities. They were capable and good problem solvers possibly, but alone and often lonely.

Yellow Zone children are like kites flying loose – free and detached.

I recall a story of a young woman who graduated top in her university class. She completed law school and practiced law in a large city. She was successful and a survivor in a difficult legal establishment. She, however, did not feel valued or needed. She eventually began robbing banks. She liked knowing that at least the police were looking for her. Being competent alone is not enough. Dorothy Briggs in *Your Child's Self Esteem* tells us that being competent and being loved are necessary for a child's self esteem. Being competent and being loved are aspirations for all ages.

Reflection:

Missing in Action

Some parents appear to be Missing In Action. In my neighborhood, children are fighting a war. Although I do not live in the Middle East, thoughts of that conflict come to mind as I watch with dismay what younger children consider fun. The game includes shoving, pushing, as well as other behaviors that I would call bullying and hurtful talk by older children. Children sneak around trees, yell obscenities and shoot one another. The combatants own large, expensive water guns that look like something used in the filming of "Saving Private Ryan."

Parents of these children appear busy with something else. These parents appear to me to be missing. I have been astonished to watch this form of play ignored by parents. These are the same parents who read about violence and bullying behavior in the newspapers and demand teachers and school administrators be vigilant and assure safety in the classroom.

The neighbor children's language, actions and verbal threats disturb me. I work in a school district where such language is inappropriate. School board members do not allow guns and have implemented "zero tolerance" into the policy. I recall a Los Angeles riot where a beaten and bloodied black man asked the ever-present CNN camera, "Can't we get along?" Disguised as game players, the children on my block are practicing how not to get along.

After a full day of teaching, I stopped at a fast food restaurant to buy some coffee. Parents waiting for food stood mesmerized by the large lighted menu complete with pictures and prices. The children, meanwhile, ran around the tables and chairs. One boy opened all of the cold drink spigots, watching the soda splash on the floor. Everyone laughed and joined in. Children jumped up and down on corner chairs and tables, pushing and shoving each other. Some of the children started to cry while the accompanying adults stared at the picture board focused on the pictures of fries and malts. Why weren't the adults involved with their children?

Recently, a principal from a prestigious private school contacted me, concerned about the bullying behavior exhibited in the fifth grade. She wanted me to speak to the students and tell them to stop. I refused. I did, however, offer to speak to the parents. I reminded her that whatever happens in the home is twice as important as anything else in determining school success up to the age of 14. What are the key adults in their lives doing? What behaviors are acceptable in the home and neighborhood? What happens at the kitchen table? She hung up.

Where are the adults? Why are they looking away? Why are we ignoring behavior that is not OK? Parents are not only obliged to feed and shelter the young, but they also need to teach them self-control, civility and a meaningful way of interacting with the world.

These lines by an unknown author come to mind: "You're afraid of me. I throw things. I hit people. You pretend not to see. I talk back and you do nothing. You never tell me what I should or shouldn't do. You're afraid of me. And I'm scared. Please, please tell me where to stop. Don't be afraid of me."

Children who are afraid often act out. Violent and bullying behaviors are bred in the corners where fear and silence lurk. Fear lurks in my neighborhood. It is in the fast food restaurants where some children are shoved, pushed and tormented while adults look away.

Ada

Chapter 7

Red + Yellow + Green =
Purposeful Parenting

"I long to put the experience of fifty years at once into your young lives, to give you at once the key of that treasure chamber every gem of which has cost me tears and struggles and prayers, but you must work for these inward treasures yourselves."

Harriet Beecher Stowe

"I am not afraid of storms, for I am learning how to sail my ship."

Louisa May Alcott

The Yellow Zone needs to be nestled within the Red and Green Zones based on the child's age and development. Yellow, in relationship to the Red and Green, is the "you are trusted" zone. When the Yellow stands alone it feels like "I am not important enough to be noticed" or "I don't matter." The key is the relationship among all three. In the model, the Yellow Zone is the zone in which parents observe. The child has power and the opportunity to explore and make choices. The child's behavior, however, is monitored. If the child chooses to steal, he or she has moved into the Red Zone. Participating in dinner conversations, helping with chores and smiling in the morning are but a few of the Green Zone possibilities. A two-year-old choosing to wear a ballet dress for three days is a Yellow Zone decision for me. Other parents might be disturbed by having a twirling two-year-old. Wearing a ballet dress for a few days is not an infraction of family rules or limits. It is something that the child enjoys and finds pleasure in controlling. Other parents might be quite troubled by this clothing choice. Parents need to decide what is acceptable or unacceptable in the home. That is included in the parent's job description.

The difficult part of the Yellow Zone concept is keeping in mind the child's age. Assisting in a video selection for an 8-year-old is a different dynamic from when the child is 16. One could argue that a parent's influence over a 16-year-old's actions is, in fact, minimal. For that reason, early learning and clarification of the three zones and how they interact is crucial. Early learning and clarification can lead to prevention. Parents can use the words "Red," "Yellow" and "Green" to promote family understanding. For example, in our family, violent videos are a Red Zone. We will not have them in our house. For our family, eating dinner in the living room is unacceptable. That is a Red Zone. We eat at the table with the television off. That is how our family operates. That is our Green Zone. Children selecting which clothes to wear to a party is a Yellow Zone choice. Talking about the zones with children when they are young creates opportunities for purposeful conversations. Talking about the zones is like preparing the foundation, carefully packing for the canoe trip or drinking plenty of water before a long hot race. Begin early and plan ahead.

Parents provide an allowance to teach money management. Providing an allowance is parent-orchestrated;

however, the opportunity for learning about money occurs in the Yellow Zone and the child is the primary learner. Because the child is a family member, he or she receives a sum of money each week. This allowance is not connected to household chores or rewarding behavior. Giving an allowance allows for learning at home and in the community. Children who receive a no-strings-attached allowance are operating in the Yellow Zone. "No strings" does not mean buying something that is a Red Zone family value. Should the child want to buy a pornographic movie, he or she has moved into the Red Zone. Such a purchase would not be appropriate.

My daughters saved their own money to buy Barbie dolls, something I chose not to purchase for a variety of reasons. However, when my daughters bought Barbie and all of her accouterments, I watched and sighed. There really was nothing dangerous, illegal or harmful about Barbie. Barbie purchases were my daughters' Yellow Zone right. When our daughters were older, they wanted expensive jeans. I recognized their desire for the expensive clothes as a Yellow Zone area. I, however, was not going to spend that much for them to have name brand outfits. We discussed needs versus wants and we purchased one leg and zipper while Heather and Elizabeth used their allowances to purchase the other pant leg, thus getting the jeans they wanted. We did the same thing with bicycles. We bought Elizabeth a three-speed Schwinn. She wanted a five-speed. She paid the difference between the three- and five-speed and rode the bike up and down the street, proud of her purchase. With her allowance savings she was able to get what she wanted. The transaction was not a flat "no." It did not end with no bicycle purchase. It ended with all three zones connected in a conversation that increased Elizabeth's sense of self-decision making and self-purchasing power.

A young woman wanted an expensive prom dress. Her parents would not pay for it. She had a garage sale of her old toys. She added the money from the sale to the amount her parents were willing to pay. She thought she was the belle of the ball in a dress she loved. Her mother never said a word to her daughter, but shared her struggle with the toy sale with me. She knew, however, the toys were her daughter's possessions to do with as she chose.

Buying stamps at the post office while a parent stays in the car is a Yellow Zone experience. The child learns how to stand in line, ask for needed items, make change and return to the car. Perhaps this is a small event, but the child will get a sense of being trusted, capable and able to do a family errand. Selecting the menu and the guest list for a birthday party reinforces whose party it is. Having a conversation about how many may be invited, where the party where be held, and how long it will last are the Red and Green parameters that are provided by the parent.

At a holiday family dinner, a 16-year-old wanted the drumstick. She was told harshly by her grandmother that she couldn't have it. Everyone got angry and tempers flared. What's wrong with a drumstick? That would fall into the Yellow Zone for me. For the grandmother, the drumstick was in the Red Zone. The child's parents said nothing. While biting their tongues, they screamed inside.

In a hundred years, who will care if the girl ate the drumstick? The memory of a family gathering which ended in a shouting feud, however, will cling for years.

Red and Green Zone discussions vary depending on the child's age. As children age, their options increase and parental power decreases. That is why early involvement and Yellow Zone discussions are so important. The child starts to practice and learn within the safety of the home environment. The child has some experience in being in the driver's seat, albeit in a small car on a back road.

The Yellow Zone is about competency and trust. Parents can arrange opportunities for practice. Once the guidelines are clear, the parent stays out of the situation. The Yellow Zone is the space in which each child's individual traits and special interests can be celebrated. The Yellow Zone is about exploration, curiosity and self-discovery. Celebrating the Yellow Zone by a parent requires permitting the child to take a certain amount of risk. Children who choose their own clothes make interesting choices. Children who plan dinners may set the table in a unique manner. Children learn from such experiences. Children can thrive when they are encouraged to stretch their abilities and learn from the consequences. The Yellow Zone is often a challenge for parents. Children delight in it.

In the Red • Yellow • Green Framework, the Yellow Zone does not include anything which will kill, injure or prove to be illegal. An elementary school child can choose to bring home friends, but with certain expectations clearly stated in advance. For example, parents need to be present, food prepared, activities selected and the friends' parents notified. Selecting library books, deciding which shirt to wear, and determining where and when studying will occur, are all Yellow Zone possibilities. Yellow Zone options include planning a birthday party and inviting friends of the child's choice. One family had their four-year-old make dinner once a week. The menu choice was usually tortillas, cheese and chopped tomatoes. In this family, preparing dinner was a Yellow Zone decision for their son. Although parents were nearby and ingredients purchased, the freedom to make a dinner for the family was the four-year-old's. Such a choice may not be an option in other homes; however the four-year-old flourished in his home.

Yellow Zone choices depend on the Red • Green family "way." The elegance of the Red • Yellow • Green Framework is just that. Ideas can be translated to fit individual family rules, routines and expectations. The zones are a framework for family members to use to think about how they want the family to live and relate. The zones act as a compass keeping everyone moving not only together but in the same direction. Using this framework avoids losing each other along the way.

Giving children some power over their lives diminishes resistance to the parent-determined Red Zones and conveys a message that children can make choices that parents accept, respect and reinforce. I believe the ultimate power of the powerless is disruption. The Yellow Zone is a child's opportunity to claim some power over his or her life. In the Yellow Zone the sense of being trusted to make good and wise decisions is taught, practiced and learned. Children need acceptance and recognition. Acceptance occurs in the Yellow Zone. Recognition is integral to the connections between the Red and Green.

Reflection:

Daily Living of Core Values

In order to instill core values such as caring, honesty, respect and trust, values need to be part of everyone's everyday – in the kitchen, on the lawn, while running errands in the car, etc.

Children are in school nine percent of the time, according to the University of Minnesota; other "teachers" fill the remaining 91 percent of their lives. We know that home messages are powerful and long term. We also know that children do not learn merely by reading beliefs hanging on the wall. Children are quick to connect attitude and behaviors. They comment when actions do not match mandates. We know children are always watching what, when and how parents live their values. The trouble with core values is just that. They need to be core. Core values are not external, tangible, purchasable things. To be effective and credible, they need to be what breathing is to life.

Living core values is a lifetime choice. I think John Lennon wrote, "Life is what happens to you while you're busy making other plans." Although considerable time and effort can be spent on house construction, there is no guarantee that a home will be created.

Children get mixed up when daily family life clashes with what parents say they value. Many adults tell their children that they value love and relationships, but are too busy being busy to take time for those relationships. What do caring, honesty, respect and trust look like in a home? When they are present, it is a home with "I love you," hugs, and affirmations. There is time for family meetings where individual family members share their fears, frustrations, celebrations and things-to-do lists. There is no name-calling, sarcasm or hitting. Each family member would be responsible for the family work and family fun.

Respect is valuing privacy, avoiding gossip and communicating without secrecy. Trust develops over the long haul. While not available as a quick fix at the take-out window, trust prevails when parents say "I will be there" and they are, day after day after day. Trust develops when parents are consistent with rules, praise and consequences. Honesty abounds in homes where adults are mature enough to recognize that they need to be friendly adults, not a child's best friend. Care is demonstrated by cheerleading as family members chase dreams. Care and respect are evident when individuals can make decisions, plan personal events and participate in conversations without fear of being wounded.

Time is critical. Spending time with each other, not avoiding or ignoring each other, is valued and purposeful. Time is shared so all feel safe – emotionally and physically. Time for listening is a priority. Core values are present in a home when individuals handle themselves with their heads and handle others with their hearts. Preaching core values is not effective. Practicing and living them is.

Ada

RED • YELLOW • GREEN FRAMEWORK

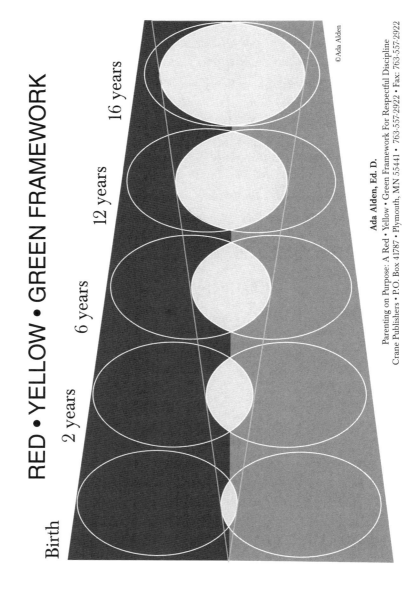

Birth   2 years   6 years   12 years   16 years

©Ada Alden

Ada Alden, Ed. D.
Parenting on Purpose: A Red • Yellow • Green Framework For Respectful Discipline
Crane Publishers • P.O. Box 41787 • Plymouth, MN 55441 • 763-557-2922 • Fax: 763-557-2922

72

Chapter 8

Red • Yellow • Green Zones:
Application Ages Birth to 2

"To storm a beach, conduct an embassy, govern a people: these are brilliant actions; to scold, laugh and deal gently and justly with one's family and one-self ... that is something rarer, more difficult, and less noticed in the world."

Montaigne

"The strongest and most influential memories are almost always those of my childhood."

Fyodor Dostoevsky

Implementing the Red • Yellow • Green Framework requires a long-term view coupled with the immediate short-term day-to-day experiences of family life. Important to the overall application is the age of the child and the family life experiences at any given point in time. During times of transition such as family moving, long parent absence, school changes, job loss, storm damage or a new baby, whatever the child's age, the Red • Green Zones need to be consistent and predictable. These parent-determined expectations, the clarification of "This is how we do it," will provide solace during stress-filled times. The Red • Green Zones give a sense of stability during times of disequilibrium.

The relationship between the zones as well as the parent role and influence change over time. The Yellow Zone changes as the child ages. As the child matures and grows into a more responsible role, the Yellow Zone increases. Although the Red and Green are always present, as the child ages, parental say over choices and options diminishes. This framework is designed to help parents select a road map, a course that will provide reassurance and a sense of direction. Life events often get in the way of family planning. However, having a reasonable plan is reassuring and helps parents stay the course. Planning opportunities are integral to the family meeting described later in the book.

All of the zones must be interconnected to provide a sense of security and attachment. The Red • Green are adult-determined and reinforced. They are teaching strategies. A parent can clearly say, "Taking your brother's truck is not allowed in our home." Truck-taking is in the Red Zone. Sharing trucks, however, is in the Green Zone. Sharing trucks will give the child a sense of parent approval and reassurance. Truck-taking, on the other hand, leads to parent interference and discussions about appropriate behavior. Bookstores are filled with books on behavior management strategies, consequence tactics and suggested ways to reinforce behavior. Parents can make prudent choices from these sources to use effectively within the Red • Yellow • Green Framework.

The Red • Yellow • Green Framework can be likened to a clothes closet. It provides a place to hang different strategies, activities and communication ideas. The closet is arranged in three sections. Are these Green reinforcing ideas? Is this a Red "no" in our house? Thoughtful reading of the many parenting strategy books will help a concerned parent select which ideas fit in their own Red • Yellow • Green Framework. I recall reading an idea by a parent expert who thought pinching a child was an efficient parenting strategy that did not leave a mark on the skin. For me, the "pinch" would not be something to hang in my Red • Yellow • Green parenting closet. A pediatrician told a worried mother to put a board over the crib to keep an exploring two-year-old contained. Boards on cribs also fail to fit in my Red • Yellow • Green world. Parents need to be prudent. Remember, as the child ages, the sizes of the Red, Yellow and Green sections change as well. Truth is, some of the early effective strategies have become ingrained behaviors. They have become "the way we do it."

The Yellow Zone may be different for each child. It is tied to a child's developmental age. However, the framework is most useful when there is consistency between parents when implementing the family Red • Green Zones. Even in a one-parent household, consistency is vital. Children who grow up without consistent "yes" and "no" concepts do not develop a sense of the North Star or an internal compass. Parents who choose not to be clear and consistent often relinquish the leadership role appropriate for the adults in the home. Too often I have seen the results of no message or inconsistent messages on a child. Either the child needs to be the leader, or he or she behaves differently depending on who is in the room. Parental consistency about what is welcomed and what is a non-negotiable provides that emotional security in which children flourish. It's helpful for young ones to know they don't have to run the household. They can relax and focus their energy on growing up.

I remember my sigh of relief when David came home and would share the parenting load. I remember waiting to hear the garage door go up. I remember gleefully shouting, "There he is." It didn't occur to me that he might have had a complicated day. Particularly when the children were young, someone else singing the "Wheels on the Bus" or someone else changing a diaper was respite. David smiled when he saw Heather. There were moments during the day when some of my smiles faded. He liked to read her stories and spend time with her. Often the selected bedtime I had practiced fell to the wayside and game playing and kite flying took precedence. Bedtime could be delayed because he had not spent father-child time. All of the day-to-day organization I had put in place ceased to exist when David came home. Heather was learning that when her father was home, things were different. As parents we were not consistent with our expectations. Heather was confused and so were her parents.

We argued, disagreed and struggled with what mattered in our daily lives. We worked hard on being clear and consistent and slowly came up with the rituals and routines that worked for us. To this day, I think the time we invested in coming to some family philosophy has paid high dividends. It is one of the reasons we are still married. Children add stress to a marriage and can cloud the value of the couple to each other. Happy marriages can be derailed when conversation and disagreements are replaced with silence, apathy and avoidance. Infants change the family dynamic at birth. Change requires substantive conversations.

It is important to define what is the parent way. The parent way is different from being the father or the mother. David is a very involved father. He enjoys fishing, game playing and taking children on adventures. I don't like fishing and think reading books aloud is better than eating ice cream, and museums are far more interesting than stadiums. The Red and Green Zones are not about making mothers and fathers the same. The Red and Green Zones define and clarify the parent role.

A consistent pattern of behaviors provides the young child with a sense of security and reliability. It provides the foundation for emotional intelligence.

For a young child, changing and discovering, understanding or exploring something new is part of every day. Change, both positive and negative, is stressful. So, if the child's every day is different, it is up to the parents to implement predictable experiences that ease anxiety.

The Red • Green Zones include the rituals and routines of how we do things. Children want and need to learn that. They like knowing how things are done. Knowing seems to act as a stress reducer for children. It is the parent's job to clarify the family Reds and Greens. This establishes a sense of predictability and trust. If the rituals and routines of a home are six movies and popcorn on the weekend, I think the message is "We know how to avoid each other." The lesson is "Time together is television driven." If, however, the weekend always includes the family members cleaning the house together and sharing a game after dinner, the message is "We as a family know how to work and play together." All routines teach something. What are the lessons children are learning? Parents are at-home teachers who need to pay attention to the day-to-day curriculum of their lives.

Consider these suggestions and add your own.

Red • Yellow • Green Suggestions

Age	Red NO	Yellow MINE	Green YES
	parent determined	child determined	parent determined
Birth–2	leaving child alone in tub	walking	setting bedtime routine
	eliminating access to dangerous items	crawling	using infant car seat
	securing entryways	deciding amount of food eaten	stimulating five senses
	_____	eliminating body fluids	assuring movement
	_____	_____	providing verbal interaction
	_____	_____	_____

In the first years of life, parental decisions are primarily about the Red and Green Zones. Children need to be kept safe and assured they are loved. A relationship with a caring, supportive adult is heavily weighted as a protective factor. Children need to learn at an early age that when they have needs, someone will be there for them. Babies who are cared for mature into self-regulating human beings. A clear Red and Green Framework in the early years establishes connections from which a thoughtful Yellow Zone can emerge as the child ages.

At birth, the Yellow Zone is about reading the child's cues. Infants communicate needs and wants at birth. Parents are responsible for the child's safety and care. However, babies are in charge of when they eat, sleep or release body fluids. The Yellow Zone for a crawler is a parent who, albeit watchful, welcomes the child's eagerness to explore.

Parents and caregivers need to have discussions about simple safety. Children cannot be left alone in the bathtub. Car seats must be used or the car does not go. Sharp objects, open stairways, medicine cabinets and electric outlets are but a few hazards that easily attract a small child. Children mimic the adults they observe. Razors need to be put out of reach. Bookshelves look like something to climb. Cleaning materials, even those marked with a poison sticker, are still unsafe. Put them away. Take care that little ones don't climb out of their beds and wander outside. Children learn quickly how to open doors, turn keys and grab forbidden items. The Red Zone for the very young child is really life saving.

Many wonderful books emphasize the importance of loving a child. Reading stories daily, saying "I love you," and being physically and psychologically present for the young child are the Green Zone. Assuring the child has consistent bedtime and mealtime routines is core to parenting in a purposeful way.

Reflection:

Lessons from the Canada Goose

The Canada goose family is fascinating. Presently many family clusters inhabit the neighborhoods through which I run. Both adults are flightless after goslings are born. While regrowing flight feathers, Ma and Pa Canada Goose are always available, walking one in front and one in back of their goslings. When under pressure, the family unit stands together. Shared family events are never a question; parents can't get away. Sharing the parenting role comes with the Canada Goose package.

In our too busy world, we perhaps should reflect on the value of being physically and psychologically available to our children. Parental availability, according to all the research, is critical in the development of a sense of self-worth and emotional well-being in young children. Actually, a child's relationship with parents – the sights, sounds, smells and feelings they experience as well as the challenges they meet – not only influences their moods but actually affects the way a child's brain becomes "wired." The everyday moments of simple, loving encounters provide essential nourishment for the brain. This nourishment is necessary for neurons to grow and connect with other neurons in systems that control various functions like seeing, hearing, moving and expressing emotion. Early experiences help determine brain structure, thus shaping the way people learn, think and behave for the rest of their lives. Canada Geese act like they have read the research.

It is necessary to schedule daily shared interaction with our children, with one another. Outside intruders like TV, videos, over-scheduled calendars, need to be held at bay. Learning nursery rhymes and reading stories should take priority over IRA's, mall sales and fast food joints. Staying with young children is not always easy, nor do we always know what to do. Yet, our kids are just learning, too. Adult silence, adult distancing, adult unavailability all confuse children. At the end of a busy workday, whether at home or at a place of employment, it would be smart to remember the Canada Goose. I believe we need to be wary of overusing our flight feathers. Maybe we, too, should walk with our goslings more often.

Ada

Chapter 9

Red • Yellow • Green Zones: Application Ages 2-6

LETTING ME HELP
is letting me share your world,
letting me practice.
Dissolving ever so slowly
walls between worlds of a child
and yours.
Letting me help is letting me
feel important
and needed.
Wanting to grow up ...
to be like you.
Ruth Reardon - Listening to the Littlest

The two-year-old requires important consideration of all the three zone colors by the parent. The Yellow Zone is a place of celebration for the two-to-six year-old. The expanding Yellow Zone can be a source of frustration for the parent. "Let me do it" is the central melody with a supporting theme of "mine." It is a wonderful opportunity for parents to learn how to share the power in a thoughtful, selective way. It is also an important time to renegotiate and clarify what are Reds and Greens. The child is mobile, verbal and eager to discover the wonders of his or her ever-expanding world.

Red • Yellow • Green Suggestions

Age	Red NO parent determined	Yellow MINE child determined	Green YES parent determined
2 - 6	hitting	choosing clothes	clearing the table
	grabbing toys	selecting library books	sitting at the table
	throwing food	deciding amount of food to eat	using seatbelts
	breaking toys	selecting toys for play	putting toys away
	_____	_____	_____

When Heather turned two she received a fishing pole complete with a hook, bobber and tackle box. She was delighted. I worried about the hook and her eyes. My husband said he would teach her how to use the equipment. She carried the pole for years. She loved to fish and listened attentively when her father taught her how. She was in charge of her own pole, tackle box and hook if she used them within the constraints of the Red and Green Zone. Reds were "Don't take the pole and hook outside to play." The Greens were positive comments she received when fishing, baiting hooks and sitting in the boat. At two and a half, she was quite a capable angler.

When Heather turned four her father bought her a Swiss Army knife. It arrived in its own leather case complete with a scissors, awl and tweezers. Actually Heather attached it to her belt and was almost thrown off balance due to its size. I did not approve. It had not been made by a reputable toy manufacturer and certainly didn't have "appropriate for four-year-olds" written on the box. David, again, taught me about the value of the Yellow Zone. "I'll teach her how," he said. When Heather said, "I will take the knife to nursery school," that was a Red Zone. However, she could use it to help prepare dinner and on camping outings. Through the years she was reinforced for proper use of the knife and to this day uses it as an adult woman who still loves to go into the woods. The message from her father was one of trust and competence.

Yellow Zone decisions need to be tailored to and for the child involved. Giving Heather a knife at four was work-able for her. There are many who should not be using a knife as adolescents. Each child is unique and reading the cues will provide good guidance to caring adults in his or her life. Purposeful parenting is paying-attention parenting.

Before children enter kindergarten much learning occurs. Actually the first years of life are more significant for long-term academic success than we earlier believed. Learning does not begin in kindergarten. Young children are very capable and eager to participate. They can learn early to say "please" "thank you" and "may I come in?" Children thrive on being reassured that clearing the table, using seat belts and putting toys away are how things are done. Pre-kindergarten is an important time to learn about feel-ings and what to do when you are feeling angry, frustrated or sad. Parents need to remind children consistently that hitting is not acceptable.

When Elizabeth was two, a sign on our refrigerator said, "No Hitting." She used to welcome visitors to our home by saying, "You can come in, but there is no hitting in our house." The children learned quickly that before friends could go home, puzzles had to be put away. They were the only ones who knew where the puzzle pieces went, I might add. Reinforcing putting puzzle pieces away, as well as interactions that do not include hitting, is the teaching opportunity present in the Green Zone.

Grabbing toys away from each other was not the way to get what they wanted. For years, we talked about asking, trading, sharing and allowing toys to be played with on loan. Children like to play games. Children do not like to put games away. Games needed to be put away in the their storage boxes. The family rule was whoever won had to put the game away. That somehow eased the pain of losing.

This is a wonderful time to begin the Yellow Zone opportunities. Young children two and older are eager to have some power over their lives. Choosing their own clothes is a good place to begin. Sometimes after a child selects what to wear, it is helpful to add a nametag that says "I dressed myself." This tag will bring welcome smiles.

Parents can choose what food is brought into the home. I don't think, however, you can force a child to eat. The atmosphere at mealtime and what food is present are parent-determined. Eating, however, is the child's choice.

When children came to play at our house, Elizabeth and Heather were able to choose which toys to share and which toys they wanted to keep safely in their rooms. Such toy selection gives a child a sense of control and teaches a lesson about ownership and sharing. Using a timer may be helpful. Playing with a toy can be limited to five minutes. When the timer rings, the toy is handed to the other child. I recall two-year-olds holding a truck, staring at the timer, waiting for the bell to ring. As soon as the bell rang, the truck was handed over to the other child who also stood staring at the timer. The lesson of give and take can be taught at an early age.

We lived near a library when Heather was small. We walked to the library three times a week. She had her own card and delighted in selecting her own books from the children's section. She had her own book bag and felt quite responsible as she lugged her books home. Today she is an avid reader and member of three book clubs. I believe it all started when she was three years old.

Reflection:

Take Time to Simmer

My mother cooked spaghetti sauce all day on the back of the stove. Ingredients were always fresh and added at the proper time. My mother understood slow simmer until done. My mother was not a sauce-in-a-jar problem solver. "Some things take time," she assured me. Some things are not "flash in the pan," do it "quick and easy" deals. Conscientious parenting requires simmer practices.

We seem to be living in a let's hurry and microwave our way through life track. We are hurrying our children and their growth process. We dress them up like adults too soon. We want them to earn money too soon. We want them to be involved in organized sports too soon. We want to teach reading and math too soon. Children today are not really much different developmentally from those who slogged through the mud with their parents on covered wagons heading west. The times are expressway driven, but our children still ache for a sandbox way of life.

We know good stuff about children. We know two-year-olds cannot share. They will share only after they know what they possess. Three-year-olds are just learning about words in sentences. Three-year-olds will only learn how to talk if they are included in conversations. Too many young children are learning how to fight from television wrestlers, not how to talk from caregivers. We know four-year-olds can't always tell the truth. Four-year-olds, by definition, are fanciful, fantasy-loving make believers.

Six-year-olds show extremes in behavior. They laugh and cry easily, loving one minute and being hostile in the next. Elementary school children not only need to learn how to talk, but when and what is appropriate to say. Adolescents first must be self-centered before they can be other-centered. Other-centeredness comes only after adolescents have figured out who they are and how and where they belong.

Too many adults are hurrying the process. They want to adultify their children so their behavior might be better understood. It is easier to understand people when they are just like us. Children aren't like us. Children are still in process. I wish more adults would recognize that children need time to simmer. Children should be respected and accepted. Marva Collins, the pioneering Chicago educator, said, "We want brilliant children, but we don't want to spend the time creating them." My mother knew about time. Kids and good sauce need to simmer.

Ada

Chapter 10

Red • Yellow • Green Zones: Application Ages 6-12

"Parental love is as natural as rain; parenting skills need to be taught."
William Raspberry - Washington Post

"Submit to the rule you laid down."
English Proverb

In the elementary years, children and most parents become actively involved in a school system. The system provides teachers other than parents and caregivers, and a school curriculum that includes language arts, mathematics, social studies and more. These years offer parents an important opportunity to support learning at school and at home.

The Red • Yellow • Green Framework lends itself well to this exciting educational experience. For parents, one Green Zone suggestion is to provide an allowance. The allowance is intended to teach money management. The lessons gained through an allowance are many. Certainly using addition and subtraction are basic. Parent discussions about finances help encourage financial application. For example, dinner conversations about saving money for vacations or to purchase an item, or about using coupons teach budgeting at an early age. Older children

Red • Yellow • Green Suggestions

Age	Red NO parent determined	Yellow MINE child determined	Green YES parent determined
6 - 12	paying for chores	deciding how allowance is spent	giving allowance
	damaging books	choosing books	reading books aloud
	leaving without telling destination	choosing sports	writing thank you notes
	trick or treating late	choosing friends	joining in family work
	taking stuff without asking	choosing instrument	eating dinner together
	watching R-rated videos	wrapping gifts	being respectful of siblings
	_____	_____	
	_____	_____	_____

can help compute gas costs, car mileage and expenses that occur on a weekend trip. Figuring out meal costs on a budget helps children apply abstract numbers to concrete items such as grocery lists. Our children helped at the store using coupons and calculators to figure out which item to purchase. This is a wonderful time for children to receive a consumer magazine dedicated to young children. They can learn early about the market place and how to make thoughtful consumer decisions. Positive reinforcing of good money management teaches responsibility.

A Red Zone action would be paying children an allowance to do the chores. Chores are something everyone does. No one is paid for cleaning. Family work is as important as family play. Payment for family work undermines important lessons which working together can teach. We have, however, paid children for some unusual work in the home. Washing many apples for classroom field trips, polishing silver or washing cars were ways to earn extra money.

The Yellow Zone for allowances was letting children use the money for choices that were pleasing to them. Granted, pornographic or dangerous materials were not allowed, but certainly candy and gum were early choices. The amount of allowance provided did not permit purchasing large amounts of candy or gum. Parents may need to have a good supply of toothpaste and dental floss. Over time, our children learned about saving, earning interest, putting money in the church plate and buying family gifts with their own money. I still remember the joy on Heather's face when, with her own money, she purchased a soup ladle for her father. She beamed.

Whenever our children were reading, I was delighted. I took them to the library, bought special books for gifts and was sure they had a place to keep their books. As part of the Yellow Zone, at the library they could choose books they wanted. Books were to be treated with care and tearing pages was in the Red Zone. Books we no longer needed were carefully donated to others who had no books. Books were, and continue to be, valued in our home.

Although the elementary years offer many new opportunities for Green Zones, the ones established in younger years are maintained. Everyone still cleared the table after eating, wore seat belts and put toys away. We just didn't have to talk about these actions so often. These were learned behaviors and part of everyone's everyday routine. New skills included writing thank you notes, joining in family work and preparing meals together. Our family established a family meeting routine during these elementary years. We met weekly, followed Roberts' Rules of Order, kept minutes, and eventually learned how to communicate. The "how" and "why" of family meetings is explained in detail later in this book. I have found the meeting to be essential in learning and practicing family rules, family connections and family expectations. Family meetings add vitality and practicality to Red • Yellow • Green thinking.

We had two children and they were expected to be respectful of each other. We didn't expect them to like each other. Actually, for years they didn't. I remember teaching them how to fight. Fighting did not include hitting. We worked hard to learn how to argue gently. Refresher courses are still helpful. Having a clear time to be home was in the Red Zone. Being late or roaming the streets was well situated in the non-negotiable Red Zone.

Getting home on time was a reinforced Green Zone. Other Red Zone designees included no trick-or-treating past 8 p.m. or going alone house to house. Leaving without telling, taking stuff without asking or watching "R" rated movies was not OK at our house.

Our children had different Yellow Zone options because of their age difference as well as their very different likes and dislikes. As children get older this Zone gets more complicated. Both girls took swimming lessons. They were expected to learn how to swim. Becoming good swimmers was a Green Zone expectation. A Red Zone action would have been to refuse to learn how to swim. I have always believed equipping children with good life skills is a parent's responsibility. For us, teaching children to swim is important and necessary. Both of our children are good swimmers. I never worried when they went canoeing into the wilderness on camping trips. I knew they knew how to get to shore if necessary. They did not have to learn how to ice skate, however. One took lessons for years; the other wanted no part of it. They chose sports they wanted. Our job was to get them there and home in a timely manner. Elizabeth wanted to play the French horn. That was a challenge. Getting the horn to and from school was far more difficult than it would have been had she chosen a flute.

Being a friend and learning how to discern good friends can take years to learn. Our children selected their own friends. Some were quite unusual and not my choice. However, friend selection was located in the Yellow Zone. It would have been a mistake to suggest certain friends were not allowed. That statement can easily backfire. Soon that individual could become the most sought-after relationship. In the elementary years, children should practice and experience how to be with friends. Although friend selection in the elementary years is the Yellow Zone, parents can monitor, provide popcorn and provide rides. During these times relationships with friends and encouraging positive interactions can occur. Parents who are present and monitoring activities complete the Red • Green Framework. It was interesting to me to notice how some friends slowly disappeared from birthday parties after a daughter decided the friendship wasn't a fit. Had we openly disapproved of that friend, the child might still be coming to parties.

Our children used to ask what to wear to an event. I would dutifully tell them. They would then come out proudly wearing something else. Actually, Heather once told me how she loved my telling her what to wear. Then she knew to choose something else. I quickly learned to say, "You will make a good choice." Heather learned how to select clothes and find a look that suited her. The Yellow Zone needs to be age appropriate. I remember when Elizabeth wanted to mow the yard. She was only eight and mowing was not an option. When she got older, and it would have been a wonderful idea, her interest had waned. Mowing the lawn moved into the family chores right along with dumping trash, making beds and washing dishes.

Careful consideration of the three zones during the years six to 12, prepares all family members for communication and connection during adolescence.

Reflection:

Strong-Necked Condors

Recently, condors were considered to be an endangered species. Fear of their extinction disturbed Audubon members and ornithologists throughout the country. Condor eggshells are thick and somewhat scaly. Baby condors need to pick and bang their heads vigorously in order to break the shell prior to being hatched. Worried bird lovers eased the pecking process by assisting in shell breaking. They believed by helping condors hatch, more would survive, resulting in an increased bird count. The escape from the shell was made easier, resulting in baby condors that not only failed to thrive, but also died. The struggle prior to birth helped the condors develop stronger bodies.

No struggle = no endurance and no longevity

We are raising children who are being helped to death. Adults who do too much for their children do so in the mistaken belief they are easing their way. They want children to be happy. We try to help by pointing out the "better way." Parents are buying the "best," meeting demands, and jumping buildings at a single bound to assure their child gets it, makes it and does it. Over indulgence slowly moves along the continuum of "I'll do it for you" to a child thinking, "I can't do it."

We are raising children who move into young adulthood avoiding challenges, not completing their work, and demonstrating a pattern of self-indulgence and lack of discipline. We are not raising strong-necked condors.

Maria Montessori told us this years ago. "Never help a child with a task at which they can succeed on their own." The important news has to be this: Don't protect your children from struggle, sweat and difficulty. Important lessons come from being responsible for one's own journey. That does not mean children shouldn't be cherished, celebrated and encouraged. It does mean, however, there is merit in standing back and respecting each individual's life journey. Don't take away the right to learn, to grow, to regroup and bang your head once in awhile. Condors learn early about being in charge of their own destiny and figuring things out themselves.

Condor count is up. The California skies are filled with high-flying, strong-necked birds. That is hopeful.

Ada

Chapter 11

Red • Yellow • Green Zones: Application Ages 12-16

WHAT ARE YOU SAYING ABOUT THE WORLD
when you shield me too tightly?
What are you saying about me
when you don't let me go?

Am I hearing that life is dangerous?

Am I hearing that I can't make it?

LET ME LOOK AWAY
and see that there are others
Let me move away
for there are others.
Important as you are,
and will remain,
Let me look away
for there are others
for us both.
Ruth Reardon - Listening to the Littlest

Children in early adolescence focus their energies on relationships, activities and experiences outside of the home. As always, it is important for parents to be available and aware. Between the ages of 12 and 16, many communication skills practiced in the elementary years

Red • Yellow • Green Suggestions

Age	Red NO parent determined	Yellow MINE child determined	Green YES parent determined
12-16	talking on the phone after 10 p.m.	doing homework	attending family events
	having TV on while doing homework	planning birthday parties	reading books
	behaving rudely	choosing attire	attending church
	skipping school	succeeding academically	attending school
	acting disrespectfully	selecting friends	welcoming friends
	_____	_____	_____
	_____	_____	_____
	_____	_____	_____
	_____	_____	_____

are finely honed. During these years, it is a parent's job to maintain the rules and limits and it is the child's job to test them. Consider these suggestions and add your own.

Dr. William Doherty, author of many books on family living, suggests that parents be clear about what is by invitation and what is a command performance. For example, it is important that children attend grandmother's 80th birthday party, even though most 14-year-olds would not find such an event intriguing. For me, this would be an expectation and would fall into the non-negotiable category. Certainly it might be possible for a friend to accompany the 14-year-old. That is up to the values of the family. Reassuring the child that his or her attendance is welcomed, valued and expected is important. Reading books, magazines or newspapers in our home was a Green Zone. Actually copies of *Games* magazine always went with us on long trips. Crossword puzzles and other word games were part of many journeys. To this day, on family outings, books and magazines are packed first. I believe our family relationship is better because we drove without DVD's in the car. The ride was a place to talk.

During this time many religious groups offer young people spiritual guidance and study. For many this is a family expectation. I recall one mother who worried about what her daughter wore to church. The child would only wear slacks and her mother was distraught. It seemed to me that the important question was church attendance, not what was worn. Following a short conversation, the mother reframed the problem and realized what was important to her. She let her daughter wear whatever she wanted and quietly reassured her as her daughter eagerly attended services. The Green Zone was evidenced by the parent attending church with her daughter. She was modeling the importance of a spiritual practice in her daily life. The Yellow Zone can be recognized in the no comment about what the child was wearing. Going to church was the important aspect of the experience. It was not about a parent's need for a fashion statement.

By using the Red • Yellow • Green Framework a parent can better decide what is significant and what is secondary. Thinking through the Red • Green guidelines helps parents focus on what really matters. Particularly at this age, it is helpful to clarify parent life-issues and separate them from child life-issues. Parents need to hold the line on acceptable and unacceptable behavior. Foul language was and still is a Red Zone for all of us. Rude behavior was not ignored. Being angry, frustrated and miserable was accepted and even expected. How such feelings are shared is the concern. Name-calling and abusive language are Red Zones. By the same token, good manners were and are important and reside in the Green Zone. Good manners, like swimming, are necessary life skills.

Maintaining a bedtime during the school year was important. I did not want children talking on the phone into the late hours. Although difficult to manage, we monitored bedtime, had no televisions in bedrooms and tried to control phone conversations after 10 p.m. We also knew that homework needed to be completed, and television and homework were not a combined event. I remember worrying about Elizabeth, who always studied physics in the bathtub. I was not happy about that. Somehow the book stayed dry, she managed to do very well in the course and her choice of study spot was her Yellow Zone. I remember her reminding me that she wasn't watching television and liked the tub location. I decided this was not a parent life-issue and kept my mouth shut. Much of the Yellow

Zone requires parents observing silently. Now that I think about it, I wonder if my physics comprehension would have improved had I utilized the tub as a study area.

Reflection:

Rooms with Stories to Tell

David and I have moved many times. Once we traveled lightly. No longer. Now we have stuff. Our stuff is important to each of us, either separately or together. Dave's stuff has often not been important to me. I never did understand why 30 years of Consumer Reports *was necessary. Actually, I am still confused about 36 years of* National Geographic. *Our children have accumulated stuff. Their stuff is in boxes, in cupboards, and our basement is carefully stocked with stuff.*

Each home we have left – always with our stuff – finds me wandering through the rooms hearing the stories of our lives still present in the silence of the walls. In our first house, I found the fenced-in yard particularly vocal. I remember the rose bushes consumed by our dog, picnics under the grape arbor, and egg hunts on snowy mornings. The bedroom off the kitchen still held the whispers of a baby crying in a lovely wooden cradle. Another house had a particularly noisy kitchen. The echoes of family meetings bounced around the room. I remember David telling Elizabeth she could not stomp out of the room. She was the chairperson and was required to stay until the agenda had been completed. She stayed, tears and all. Hours of homework, family fights and celebrations were spent in that room. My, how many candles have flickered during those special moments in our lives!

Saturday, I was home alone. It was clean-the-house day. I had a German mother. Clean houses are ritual to me. Armed with a vacuum cleaner and Comet, I began in the children's rooms. No one sleeps there anymore. The rooms are never messy. Stuffed animals, no longer hugged, sit on shelves. Soccer trophies, college awards and prom dresses in plastic bags are now ignored. Smelly, tired and well-worn shoes wait to go to a nearby playing field.

I quietly closed the doors. Sobs came from deep inside. The sobs were not of sorrow, but of gratitude. I have been part of all of the stories. I know each chapter. Some stories bring tears, even amid the laughter.

Ada

Chapter 12

Red • Yellow • Green Zones: Application Ages 16+

"In order for children to develop a sense of importance and potency, they need to see themselves getting stronger and more skilled. They need to see themselves making a difference in the world."

Diane Gossen - Restitution: Restructuring School Discipline

Adolescence has been likened to a box of Cracker Jacks. One is never sure where the surprise is. Uncertainty and unpredictability are coupled with curiosity for the unknown. The early experiences in the Red • Yellow • Green Framework provide a helpful base for the family as children move to car keys, curfews and shopping malls.

I know that parents have little power over their children after a certain age. Actually I read that up to the age of 10, parents and children have equal power over decision-making. After a child turns 10, parental control diminishes quickly. A parent/child relationship based on parental power eventually will fail. Children grow and soon the power shifts. This is certainly evident after a child is 16. Between the ages of 10 and 16 the routines and rituals of past years are ingrained and become the "way we do things."

Red • Yellow • Green Suggestions

Age	Red NO parent determined	Yellow MINE child determined	Green YES parent determined
16+	drinking, using drugs	driving destinations	getting driver's license
	using bad language	using own money	getting summer job
	skipping school	joining extra curricular activities	volunteering
	ignoring	to obey or not to obey	getting home on time
	_____		
	_____	_____	_____
	_____	_____	_____

Parents can't make children do something they don't want to do. I recently heard of a young mother whose 15-year-old did not want to move to a different country. He took her credit card and car and headed for New York to earn money playing his guitar on street corners. Such actions were certainly not parent-supported. Parents finally found the boy five states away. He had no driver's license and had not even started to learn how to drive. Children will take off. The question is what skills and competencies have they developed through the years to support their move to independence?

The Green Zone during these years includes getting a driver's license and, in our home, providing a way to access the car. Many families purchase cars for adolescents. We never did. It might have been easier for the child to have his or her own car. We certainly spent hours arguing about who would drive and when a car might be available. We had difficult conversations about filling gas tanks, paying for insurance and assuring car availability. We did learn to share and our garage was vacant during many of our children's late adolescent years.

The Green Zone includes cheering at the soccer games – whether children play or not. I still have a note from Elizabeth when she graduated from high school thanking us for attending all of those games while she sat on the bench. Attending school conferences, reinforcing coming home at agreed upon times and providing access to volunteering activities are some possible Green Zone choices. Eating dinner together, welcoming friends and being available for conversations at all times of the day and night were Green Zones for us. I had food available so that friends would come. I liked knowing where the children were. The Red Zones fit in here as well. What went on at our house was monitored. Parents need to be around. There is no substitute for an adult presence.

Not too long ago, I was asked about leaving a 16-year-old and 14-year-old home alone for a week while the parent went to Paris. I thought it was a clear Red Zone. No doubt the children were responsible and competent; however, they may not have been able to handle difficult situations that might have arisen. It is amazing how quickly word gets around that parents aren't home.

Both our children had summer jobs. They needed to find their own jobs. That was the Yellow Zone. They also could spend the money as they chose during these years. Later, when they were in college, there was an expectation that a certain amount would be set aside for college tuition. However, during the high school years, the money they earned belonged to them. They had been getting allowances for years and had practiced money management. The Red and Green Zones included what and where they might work. Since transportation was such a problem, they needed to work someplace nearby.

During the high school years, children often work during the school year. This can get tricky. Study time, sport involvement and school activities can take a back seat to earning money for a car. What the parent needs, wants and values can be in conflict with what the children need, want and value. Earning good grades and being involved in school require time and energy as does paying for a car. It is important to discuss work and free time during the school year. Managing time, money and activities is another learned skill. Managing choices is just as important to me as learning manners and swimming. Competent parents often manage way too much and the child learns not only "I don't have to do it," but that someone else will and can. Too-skilled parents, who manage everything in their child's life, are missing out on a wonderful opportunity for the child to learn. Parents can't swim, manage manners or life issues for their children.

By the time our children were in high school, they told us when they would be home. We talked about the evening events and figured out how long they would take. Activities like going to football games, eating at a restaurant and driving everyone home were part of the mix. Our high school students would then tell us when they would be home. We trusted that they would. They were. I still laugh when I recall one of our daughters suggesting a specific arrival time and David suggesting that perhaps more time might be needed. He suggested adding an hour as transporting friends home might take more time and rushing while driving might be unsafe. He also suggested coming home early was an option.

If parents build on the Yellow Zone through the years, by the time their children get to high school they have practiced personal competency and sense of self-competency for years. The Yellow Zone was, however, a place where children made choices. If parents don't realize the value of the Yellow Zone in relationship to the other two areas, they will end up saying "no" to too many children's choices. Children learn from the choices they make and the consequences of their actions.

Parent life-issues are usually located in the Red Zone during these years. Clear expectations about school attendance, drug or alcohol use and meeting curfew expectations are but a few. Many parent experts encourage parents to be clear about what is unacceptable. However, whether the adolescent adheres to these expectations is probably an unknown. By the time the child is an adolescent, the parent's power over the child's actions is limited. If the Red Zones are ignored, at least the child will know that he or she is breaking a family rule.

As children get older, family discussions should include the zone idea. I think for elementary and middle school children to know "That is a Red Zone for us" is good teaching. Children will be able to make choices when they are in other situations, based on this family language.

Children who are armed with a clear sense of what their family believes in and stands for will not be muddy when it comes to making smart choices.

This is not to suggest that this framework will prevent dumb choices. But it does assume that when the child makes a foolish choice, he or she will have developed the capability to learn from the mistake and apply the lessons to future decision-making.

Through the years, our discussions have included tough choices about when the Yellow needed to broaden. How the girls learned to drive and used the car was an interesting stretch of the Red • Yellow • Green Framework. Deciding whether we needed cable access, what type of dog to get and what color to paint the bedroom required conversations about who should decide what. The easy questions honed our skills for the tough issues regarding spring break in Mexico, overnights at prom and financial responsibilities when college bound. I also noticed that our second born, Elizabeth, moved more quickly into the Yellow Zone. She watched her older sister and was eager to catch up. Elizabeth wept one day when she realized she would never be older than her sister. Although behind in years, she was quick to adapt strategies and behaviors to close the gap.

Being consistent and clear provides a sense of safety for children as they grow up. Being consistent and clear is hard work and I found it challenging and humbling. The times I have reconsidered, rethought and wished different actions had occurred are too many to count. The model seems to act like a rudder. Rudderless ships flounder and often sink. We have floundered but continue to stay afloat. When the water was rising, I found hanging onto a Red • Yellow • Green Framework concept lifesaving.

During life changes and moving to different communities we needed to be sure the Red and Green Zones moved with us. They do travel and have aged well. How we treat one another, how we value one another and how we try to live our lives is "The Alden Way." It has become an inner compass for all of us. There is some grace in that.

Reflection:

Emerging Butterflies

I believe many lessons are learned during difficult times. I often have said during times of turmoil, "My, we are going to learn from this." We learn from frustration and pain. Without struggle we become weak, unsure and eventually without clarity of vision.

A fine illustration comes from a story told by Catherine Feste who wrote the book The Physician Within. *The story is about a man who raised butterflies as a hobby. He was so touched by the difficulties they had in emerging from the cocoon that once, out of mistaken kindness, he split a cocoon with his thumbnail so that the tiny inmate could escape without a struggle. That butterfly was never able to use its wings.*

When Heather graduated from college, the 3,000 who attended commencement cheered, smiled and congratulated their own butterflies. As Heather strode confidently across the stage, I remembered the years she had shoved against us, checking to see if we really meant "no." I recalled saying "We don't do it that way. Our value system will not allow that to happen. It is our way to have conversations during dinner not stare at a screen. It is our way to light a candle at dinner even if it isn't Thanksgiving." We have spent a million hours holding steady. We have disagreed, shouted, cried and hugged. We have always avoided silence. We kept saying "We believe in you. We are here for you. We cannot let that happen. Not until you finish your chores. You will be responsible for that debt. Not until your homework is finished. We realize others don't have to ... but you do."

Parenting is a constant reevaluation of the ever-changing cocoon. Children emerge from many cocoons as they age. The parent's job is to pay attention to each stage and cherish the ever-changing flight patterns. Many of us at the college graduation were wearing freshly starched shirts covering up our well-used, well-worn cocoon structures. Our children were glorious in their flight, however.

Ada

Chapter 13

Red • Yellow • Green Zones:
Practice Makes Permanent

"Letting go of the dream child we imagined having and discovering the strengths and joys of the one who actually lives with us can sometimes be a very tough task. While you do not get to choose your child's temperament, you do have control of your responses. You can learn strategies that help your child to be successful, no matter what his temperament."

Mary Sheedy Kurcinka - Raising Your Spirited Child

I like the Red • Green Zones. I understand them. I am clear on issues of safety and respectful conversation. I understand the no-hitting, no-name calling, and no taking each other's stuff. There are times, however, when knowing and doing are difficult. My husband was more at ease with the Yellow Zone. From him, I learned the wonder and importance of giving children the option of making their own choices. I knew eventually they would depart and needed the opportunity to develop skills early. Children can learn how to make choices. Too often I said "no" to choices that were fine but different from my own. It is only when I figured out the value of letting the child learn, think, try, succeed and fail that I understood the necessity of all three zones working together.

Parent comfort in one zone can get in the way of the parent utilizing all of the zones together. I am a natural in the

Red. I have had to work hard to learn how to appreciate the Yellow Zone choices of my children. Truth is, Yellow Zone choices of colleagues, friends and other family members can bother me. The problem, of course, is mine. I continue to work on learning that. My husband was not raised in a Green Zone aware environment. He had to work as hard in Green awareness as I did in the Yellow. Actually, I still have to stay focused. After 30 years of parenting I often remind myself individuals will find the answers within themselves. Only my very young grandchildren need clear Reds to be sure they are safe. As they age, the Red Zone will again be my own to define for my own life choices.

When children are young, a parent can easily say, "This is your choice." "What would you like to do?" "You choose a shirt to wear." "I think you can decide how you want to spend your allowance." Buckling seat belts, going to bed on time, leaving the park, or going home from a party will not be so troublesome if the child can select clothes, choose which non-sugared cereal to eat, or decide which stuffed animal to take to the store. For an adolescent, going to visit an aging grandparent instead of visiting friends may not be so difficult if, on another day, friends are welcome for pizza and a movie.

It is also helpful to remember that when a young child learns no throwing food, no breaking toys and no hitting, these Reds remain consistent as the child ages. I think it's an emotional safety for children when they know being responsible for everything isn't their job. There is comfort in knowing the adults in their lives are making good decisions for and about them. This also allows children the early lesson that there are some things you choose, and there are some things adults choose. It's easier for an adolescent to make careful choices with an allowance if an allowance was part of his or her experience in elementary school. During the elementary years, children are more open to parent input and conversation about needs and wants. This is the training ground for later years when, developmentally, adolescents view parental input as poorly timed or inappropriate. It is very difficult for a two-year-old to live without "no's." It is very difficult for an adolescent to live with "no." Thoughtful increasing of the Yellow Zone through the elementary years eases the journey from preschool to high school.

Eventually the Red • Green Zones will become a part of how the young adult lives his or her life. The Red • Green structure becomes the template for an inner compass upon which a child may rely as he or she matures into adulthood, providing an inner sense of right and wrong and a trusted sense of connection. My experience has been, that when all zones are present, respectful discipline exists. Children thrive. Consequences for the Red Zone are less prevalent when children are reassured in the Green and the child's personal options in the Yellow Zone are welcomed.

My adult children write thank you notes, wear seat belts, say please and thank you and know how to carry on meaningful discussions. We all continue to stay in contact and know one another's whereabouts. We have always done that. There is nothing amazing about this. They have been doing these things throughout their lives. They also would not tolerate being hit. They know they deserve to be treated with respect. Hitting by others is not an option. What is learned in the home can become a way of life.

"The Intentional Family is one whose members create a working plan for maintaining and building family ties, and then implement the plan as best they can. " *William J. Doherty, Ph.D. - The Intentional Family*

Children learn what they live. The best way to practice and live the Red • Yellow • Green Framework is to apply it everyday. This framework provides thoughtful guidance for the plan about which Dr. Doherty writes. Recently a parent evaluated a presentation I made by writing, "This isn't really about discipline techniques; this is a way to think about living your life." It is a way to think, act and reflect.

Reflection:

Family Picture Albums

The other day I overheard a mother say, "We are catching every moment on a video." I wonder about that. Sitting and looking at picture albums promotes conversations with a sweetness of time. Will videos provide that sense of connecting and time to talk? Will the experience be externally driven by the length of the video? What happens if there is no electricity? What if no one can find the video among all the other DVD's? How accessible are family pictures hidden in computers? I wonder if the speed of the observation and the quality of the ensuing conversation will be determined by the viewing time?

I did do picture albums. Both children have a baby book. We all have family albums that have accumulated through the years. This is something smart I did. They should have been made from steel ... but they are grand. Some have corners chewed by puppies who were aging too slowly in our home. Others have had their pages turned so often they are a little loose in the hinges. Through the years, during times of transitions from nursery school to elementary, from junior high to high school, friends and acquaintances were invited over to stare at the picture albums. There were giggles. The pictures of Dave and me before children always bring squeals of laughter. My hair was funny. In quiet moments, each of us can go down and regroup, remember and review shared moments.

My children are older now. Moments together are always noted, always celebrated. Our lives are busy and our days are filled with traffic and different zip codes. The picture albums are still there. They recorded our adventures. I can look through them at a leisurely pace. I can stop and recall the camping trip where Elizabeth wanted to continue playing, continue roaming, continue talking. We finally just zipped the tent corralling her within the tent and went to sleep. Picture albums don't control the time. Videos select their own time and pace. Take a few moments to create a picture album. Invest some time to record this remarkable journey called "parenting" to savor in your future. Picture albums remind each family member they have been included in important moments. Too often we only notice growth and change when pajamas are too short.

Ada

Chapter 14

Red • Yellow • Green Framework:
Personal Application

"Have patience with all things, but chiefly have patience with yourself. Do not lose courage in considering your own imperfections, but instantly set about remedying them — every day begin the tasks anew."

Saint Frances De Sales

Feeling light within, I walk.   *Navajo Night Chant*

In the Red Zone, it was critical for me not to hit. I had been hit as a child and hitting was certainly something I knew how to do. I don't recall hitting often, although it certainly came to mind. I controlled the hitting but found yelling was the replacement. When my daughters were young they used to ask me to quit yelling. I finally figured out that if I took a deep breath, I was unable to yell. I decided I would be a no-hit and no-yell person. I even learned not to slam doors. I share these accomplishments because I believe they were and are significant. I also know stopping those behaviors when my children were young paid dividends when they reached adolescence. Slamming doors, yelling and hitting damage everyone involved. Healthy family connections are eroded when such actions are part of the family dynamic. I needed to pay attention to my own misbehavior before I could ever be an effective teacher of my children.

During one of my presentations, a young mother from the Philippines sat in the front row of the auditorium and wept. She told me she never knew she didn't have to hit her children. In her culture, hitting children was the way they were parented. She worked hard to stop that behavior in herself. She would go into the bathroom and turn on the shower. Years later she gave me a beautiful shell from her village. When our paths cross, she always gives me a hug and thanks me for helping her learn that raising children did not require hitting. Another mother used to go in the closet and shut the door before she screamed. She, too, eventually learned other ways to release anger appropriately.

Also included in my personal Red Zone was not to withdraw from a difficult discussion, argument or confrontation. I was good at withdrawing. If I left the situation, I did not have to deal with it. As a child, I was often sent to my room. I liked it there. I didn't have to confront the issues. I have learned through the years to talk with the individual with whom I am having a problem. To this day, my first reaction during hard moments is to depart. I know the common human reaction when one feels threatened is either fight or flight.

During really difficult arguments, I have scheduled a short recess which included a time to reconvene. During the break time I have been able to gather my thoughts.

To leave and not face the situation became a Red Zone non-negotiable for me. I have spent years learning how to communicate anger, frustration and fear in a purposeful but non-abusive manner. There are ways to have gut-wrenching conversations and leave everyone involved whole. That continues to be my life work. Sharing feelings and concerns in a clear and direct manner is a Green Zone opportunity. I have managed intentionally to be in situations where I knew my presence was the right thing. I also know that to keep showing up takes courage. Avoidance, for me, is no longer an option.

Another Red Zone for me was to accept responsibility for how I felt in situations. I was a cheerleader in high school. I remember walking in a parade behind horses down the main street of Long Beach, California, smiling and happy. At no time did I act as if I knew I was marching in horse dung. It took me years to figure out that I could honestly say how I felt and what mattered to me without being offensive and without undermining a relationship. I need-ed to talk about the horse dung and how I felt about it. I decided that masking my reactions or ignoring inner mes-sages would be in my Red Zone. I would pay attention to how I felt, thought and reacted. Somewhere along the way, I figured out how important it was to talk with my husband about how hard it was to be a parent. I learned to say when something needed to be changed. I remem-ber discovering that I was being so busy being an avail-able mother I was losing myself. I figured out going to get a library book for me was as necessary as getting 15 pic-ture books. I also figured out that taking time to read the book instead of vacuuming was both acceptable and nec-essary.

I needed to celebrate me and pay attention to those Green Zone moments. I used to point out to family members that I hadn't yelled all week. I was excited when the grocery shopping was done. I often reminded our children how lucky they were to have me as their mother. I reassured them that they were keepers. I did not bake as all of my neighbors encouraged; however, I did make a good salad. I was able to sing easily with our children. Hugging them was not a task. I loved taking them to museums, parks and plays. I liked reading books, having picnics and going for walks. Being affectionate with our children was not a challenge.

For some, however, that is not the case. Often during a presentation, I have asked the men in the audience if they were hugged by their fathers. Most of the men say "no" or look away. One of my favorite responses was a young father who asked, "Was he supposed to hug me?" One evening, a man in the fourth row called out, "My father hugged me for the first time last week. For the first time he said 'I love you.' Then he died in the hospice of North Memorial Hospital." I asked the man if he hugged his children. He clenched his hands and with eyes filled with tears he whispered, "It is so hard." This father was raised in a home with a Red Zone that included "no hugging." I am sure he had paid rent for years, purchased pounds of hamburger and many pairs of sneakers. But he was struggling with hugging his children. A Green Zone goal for him might be, "I will hug my children." Learning that skill may be as difficult for him as it was for me to stop yelling.

The Yellow Zone might include parents sharing activities with children that the parent enjoys. Taking children on bird trips, to museums and on camping trips may all be activities that bring parents pleasure. I have watched a father happily stretched out in a field sharing his knowledge of the stars with his children. A Yellow Zone for me was getting a babysitter and going to a movie by myself when my husband was out of town. The Red • Green considerations included finding a responsible babysitter, providing suffi-

Red • Yellow • Green Suggestions
For Parenting Roles

Red NO parent determined	Yellow MINE child determined	Green YES parent determined
being child's friend	having adult friends	being a friendly adult
avoiding yelling	attending classes	acting more mature than my child
eliminating junk food	buying artichokes	being affectionate
squelching feelings	reading my own books	reading daily to my child
ignoring children	scheduling self-time	being present

cient food and guidelines for what to do with two children and letting the three of them know when I would be back. The Yellow Zone was choosing the movie I wanted to see and buying popcorn that I didn't need to share.

A good idea is to make a list of those behaviors that matter. As the adult, I had to eliminate many actions from my own behavior. I had to learn not to hit. I had to learn how to talk things out at the dinner table. I had been raised to go to my room and come out smiling. It was difficult to talk through a concern without crying or wanting to withdraw. I knew well how to duck an issue by deciding there was really nothing wrong at all. Denial was easy. I had a lot of practice in ignoring tough situations. Children will not learn how to talk out issues if parents don't model this practice. I also had to learn to use appropriate language. Swearing children were not a hoped-for outcome. So swearing adults had to be eliminated. Children will learn hitting is unacceptable only when parents refuse to hit. Children are always watching.

When I reflect on my own Red • Yellow • Green actions, reflecting promotes a habit of self-control. It teaches me that I have some power over my actions. I can control myself. I can be a responsible adult. Claiming a personal Red • Yellow • Green framework as an adult is really about being my own referee. It is about becoming the adult I hope to be. By paying attention to my own set of Red • Yellow • Green Zones, I am also working on being a better ancestor. I want to be remembered by my children and my grandchildren as a friendly adult who adored them. I don't want to be thought of as a screamer who was always somewhat frantic.

I know that positive results are more likely when I take small steps. Not hitting was a challenge. When I am angry, tired or frustrated, it is easy to forget the behavior I am trying to change. I needed to get the "thinking Ada" into the conversation. Sometimes the "I'm angry fight-or-flight Ada" would emerge in the heat of battle. I had to stop, breathe and remember my children were trying to grow up the best ways they knew how. It was my responsibility to grab hold of me and my actions. The only way I could expect children to respond and not hit, not yell and not throw things was for me to stay on the mark of acceptable behavior. I think that children need and deserve responsible adults in their lives.

Dr. Megan Gunnar, professor of psychology in the University of Minnesota's Institute of Child Development, writes about children learning how to control their behavior when there is adult scaffolding. Children need predictable environments. Children need predictable adults in their lives. Becoming a predictable adult required a hard personal look at what behavior I would and would not do. I needed to be an intentional adult to provide the scaffolding of consistent limits, expectations, routines and reassurances.

Reflection:

Breaking Cycles

A woman in her late 30s comes to parent classes, attends parent lectures, and reads parenting books. She is struggling with her role as mother. The man who attends with her comes to lectures trying to grasp what a father does. They both sit ramrod straight in the front row. Neither blinks. They want to raise their three-year-old the "right way." Financially, she and her husband are secure. Emotionally, they believe they are at risk. They also believe if they are emotionally at risk, so is their daughter.

The mother, as a daughter, was never hugged as a child. No one listened to her while she was growing up. "Girls weren't good for anything anyway!" was the message. Her brothers went to college; she ran away. The father, as a young child, was expected to be tough, to lead, and to make quick decisions. His job was to learn how to be in control and keep a wary eye on the "bottom line." He knows about trimming the fat and being shrewd. As a young man, his education was based on a no-nonsense, get yours before someone else gets it curriculum where soft-hearted was soft-headed. Presently, he is a businessman who heads a successful company with a positive fund balance. His corporate role knowledge and his sense of what is needed in the fathering role are in conflict.

They have a three-year-old who is messy, splashes water from the tub and never has her shoes tied. She thinks going to bed is a waste of time, likes to play with her parent's stuff, and giggles when her father says things sternly. They are having family meetings, eating dinner together with the television off and reading lots of stories. They hug one another, say "I love you," and are trying to believe that a too-tidy house is unhealthy for a young child.

After a parent session, the mom came up to me and said that so much of parenting feels awkward. "This is so difficult for me. It is really more comfortable to be in a house where people scream, slam doors or suffocate in silence. I feel silly trying to do these things," she says. Inventing a family for themselves is challenging work. Neither the mother nor the dad had been provided with parenting tools from their families of origin.

I assured her breaking cycles is hard work. She needs to keep on keeping on. Living in a gentle, kind and caring family atmosphere can be learned. Sometimes saying "I love you" and hugging are more difficult than learning to swim, play the piano or run a company. Being a family takes time. The parents are learning and the three-year-old is blessed.

Ada

Chapter 15

Family Meetings

"The world is so empty if one thinks only of mountains, rivers and cities; but to know someone here and there who thinks and feels with us, and who, though distant, is close to us in spirit, this makes the earth for us an inhabited garden."

Goethe

"The way to do is to be."   *Lao Tzu*

The family meeting works as a training ground for new skills as well as a place for sharing joys, frustrations and conversations. I have found family meetings to be essential. Many professionals in the field of family education have written about family meetings. Rudolf Dreikurs, H. Stephen Glenn and Jane Nelson are but a few who have looked to family meetings as a helpful connecting strategy. The Red • Yellow • Green Framework can come alive during family meetings. If conscientiously followed, I believe this strategy can be the practice field and the conference planning committee from which skilled family members emerge. Protective factors for a family include strong parental supervision, a sense of family connection and clear expectations and responsibilities understood and practiced by all. Family meetings create an environment in which such protective factors may not only be planted but where they can flourish.

Family meetings help all family members practice and

learn understanding, respect and appreciation of one another. They are a wonderful place to practice communication skills and commitment, teach problem solving skills and learn how to deal with crises and life challenges. As I look back on our family living journey, I believe one of the two best things we ever did was to have regular family meetings. The other was a no-hitting rule that applied to everyone. Our family transitions from kindergarten through college and our daughters claiming adult roles have been eased as a result of our family living experiences during hundreds of family meetings. Our present family coming and going is met with enthusiasm and pleasure because of our years of family together moments, moments with an agenda.

The family meeting is an effective way for children to learn self-discipline, leadership skills and the importance of sharing power.

The meeting is a time when all family members are seen as significant stakeholders in the family life journey. It is an experience that changes as the family matures. It, however, always has some key aspects that are consistent and predictable. Skills that emerge from having family meetings help the family when really challenging issues need to be considered. Family members learn how to problem solve, how to reach consensus and how to disagree and maintain personal dignity. A meeting promotes skill development for all. We were able to talk about really tough stuff as our children got older because, for years, we had been practicing and learning good communication skills at our family meetings. It takes a long time to learn how to swim well. Children spend years learning how to read, write and do math. Learning how to play tennis, soccer or ice skate takes hours and hours of repetition and practice. The family meeting teaches family members how to be a family for, with and to one another. Like any other skill, learning this takes practice, practice, practice.

Before family meetings can be incorporated into the calendar, it is helpful if the adults in the home agree that meetings would be worthwhile. Meetings really can be helpful for the long-term goals of family cohesiveness and connection when the adults believe they are important and necessary. Family meetings cannot be meaningful in a home if adults consider them to be fluff and trivial. I do know of some parents, however, whose partner refused to participate in the meeting; the determined parent still found meetings helpful. Children know and sense when parents don't buy into an experience. The meeting needs to be authentic with participants committed to the process.

If getting together as a family is considered trivial, the long-term outlook may be grim. After teaching the family meeting concept, I have been told by many adults that they really didn't have time to meet regularly. How can they not? Why is it that families who are in trouble and meeting with chemical dependency counselors or family therapists are told to go home and have a family meeting before returning for another session? Skilled professionals working with troubled families often ask, "When and how are you talking and working together?"

Family meetings are about developing skills to help maneuver through some of the shoals along the way. Meetings are a strategy that works in the immediate everyday of family living and provides family members training for future dilemmas. Family meetings, when children are young and when parents are just learning their role, are smart and can be fun. Meetings should be held regularly and all should be present. A family meeting is an organized meeting which results in a sense of family importance and a valuing of family function. Family meetings are a place in which common sense approaches can be practiced, taught and encouraged.

Each family member has a job at the meeting. Positions rotate to promote a sense of responsibility and capability in all. There is a chairperson, someone who writes the agenda, another who takes minutes and one who prepares the treats and eats. If there are more than four in the family, someone could select the site for the meeting, arrange the chairs and be sure necessary writing materials are available.

Early in the family meeting process, it is helpful to discuss a few ground rules. The chairperson is in charge of the meeting. Every family member has the opportunity to speak without being interrupted. I remember Heather sharing how much she liked family meetings because anyone could say whatever needed to be said without fear of being wounded. Family members are encouraged to share their feelings and concerns without name-calling or sarcasm. A family meeting needs to be an emotionally safe experience. Actually it teaches all members to practice being civil with one another.

Each family should create its own family meeting style. The following suggestions have proven effective for my family. We started when our Elizabeth was three. Our meetings continue to this day, even though our daughters are grown. My husband and I still touch base in a somewhat formal way once a week to share calendars, concerns and conversation. As I look back on some recent significant events, I realize that the skills we developed over the years holding family meetings were the very ones we used to plan a wedding, deal with my father's death and plan a large family reunion. Those were the same skills employed when housing contractors did a poor job and selection of house painters became a daunting task.

I believe it is helpful for all family members to have their own calendars. Too often one person is responsible for the family calendar. This does not help children learn how to plan or, more importantly, learn how to be aware of someone else's calendar and plans. Each year a holiday gift was a calendar for the new year. I remember fondly moving from calendars displaying cats to country scenes and then on to the Impressionist painter Monet as our children matured.

Job descriptions are helpful as everyone learns how to be involved. Remember every job rotates weekly so all learn how to perform the different roles necessary for an effective meeting.

Family Meeting Job Descriptions

Agenda Preparer

The person who writes the agenda follows a format that provides the structure for the meeting. The agenda is usually written on a separate piece of paper and made available to the chairperson prior to the meeting. Our agenda consisted of the Minutes, Schedule of the Week, New and Old Business, Finances, Problems and Issues, Jokes, Hurrahs and Boos.

Chairperson

The chairperson calls the meeting to order, follows the agenda, and is responsible for asking each family member if he or she has any comments on the agenda topics. The chairperson is responsible for enforcing the ground rules for discussion and has the right to call someone out of order. It can be quite grand for the youngest in the family to call a parent or sibling out of order. The chairperson controls the meeting, facilitates discussion and makes sure that agenda items are covered.

When my daughters attended college they were usually the president of their clubs, head of the dorm rooms and captains of teams. Separately they have commented how others did not know how to run a meeting, much less write an agenda and take minutes. They, of course, had been doing it all of their lives. Once learned, the skills can be effectively utilized for a lifetime.

Recorder

This person writes the minutes to the best of his or her ability. Some families have recorded the minutes on a tape recorder and then transcribed them. As the children grew older, their minute-taking improved. They learned quickly how to spell "business" and "agenda." I recall when Elizabeth commented that the last person who had written minutes had not done so carefully. I had been the recorder the week before and my writing was not up to snuff.

The recorder also reads the minutes from the meeting before. Initially the minutes are short but always important. Family meetings teach skills. The recorder learns to write, record and read important family events. I might add, our books of minutes are treasured. Our now-grown children have come home and read through the old minutes. We have laughed and cried together again as we look at those chronicled moments that chart the journey of our lives.

Treats and Eats

The person responsible for Treats and Eats also makes sure that the necessary ingredients are on the grocery list. The person in charge of treats and eats also prepares them. We have had some wonderful treats and sometimes they were gone too soon. Chips, cheese, salsa and vegetable dip usually made up our choices. Some of the minutes reflect the fact that our treats and eats were insufficient for the family business that week.

Other jobs could be deciding where the meeting should held, arranging the chairs, etc. We were a family of four and the jobs rotated according alphabetically by our first names.

The Family Meeting Process

The meeting should begin on time. Treats and eats are prepared in advance. All family members bring their own calendars. We have found sitting at a table or kitchen bar area worked well. We usually sat in a circle so that everyone could see everyone else when they spoke. Family meetings can go as long or as short as needed. Families with young children would do well to have a short, concise agenda. As our children got older and some of the topics got more complex, some meetings went over an hour. I look back on those shared times as an investment in our future. We took the time to be sure everyone was heard.

Call the Meeting to Order

The chairperson notes the time and date for the recorder to include in the minutes. The meeting is called to order when all are present, treats are in place and each person has a calendar and pencil.

Minutes

The recorder reads the last meeting's minutes which are written in a journal-type book. When our children were small, the youngest would often draw pictures conveying the issue. I recall the dog drawing when we were trying to decide who would walk the dog and pick up poop. Other parents have written down exactly what the three-year-old said. This, too, would capture the little one's comments and model for all at the meeting that everyone in the family had a voice and mattered.

Schedule of the Week

This is when the calendars are used to plan the whereabouts of family members. It is the time when birthday parties, soccer games, dentist appointments and out-of-town trips are shared. The first time we did the schedule of the week we discovered Heather had to be at a band practice when both her father and I were busy. She had all week to find another ride to the event. Without the family meeting and schedule of the week discussion, we would have discovered the conflict in our schedules too late. A wild and frantic unhappy time was averted. In addition, Heather learned how to plan ahead and be responsible for her own appointments.

Finances

This is the time when any extra expenses could be discussed. Allowances can be distributed and questions about needs and wants reviewed. I recall during "finances" having wonderful talks about the cost of gas, meals and lodging when we were planning a family car trip. It was during this time that the children would periodically raise the question of an increase in allowance. The allowance was not given for chores completed but given to the children because they were members of the family and needed to learn money management. Talking about the cost of electricity and air conditioning helped promote turning off the lights and closing the front door during summer. Summer lemonade stand profits as well as the cost of school clothes were included during the finance discussion. The children knew for years that we were putting money away for them to go to college. Money acumen was practiced, discussed and learned through the years.

Problems and Issues

Each family member can raise a concern or problem that can either be with another family member or with something or someone else. It is a time for all to have input, provide suggestions or problem-solve. We have had wonderful tough discussions during "P and I" as Elizabeth called it. Folding clean clothes, replacing a birthday doll whose hair had been wrongfully combed, establishing strategies for borrowing clothes and figuring out piano practice schedules are but a few that I remember. It was also an opportunity for my husband to share the challenge and pain connected with visiting his dying friend in the hospital and my struggles with job expectations, tennis players who miscalled shots and the meanness of fifth grade girls. It was during "Problems and Issues" we came to grips with the necessity of putting one dog to sleep due to old age. It was during "Problems and Issues" we talked about another of our dogs who was biting and dangerous. Heeding the veterinarian's concerns, we, as a family, made a difficult but necessary decision. We talked about prom night, trips to Mexico, alcohol and drug use, as well as how to get car insurance, visit grandparents and do laundry. Together we learned how to respectfully deal with the tough stuff and the not-so-tough stuff in "Problems and Issues."

New/Old Business

This was a time to plan picnics, provide feedback on strategies implemented to solve problems, and consider vacation options. I remember when we were on a summer vacation and the girls insisted that we keep to the meeting schedule. One of the worries was whether grandparents vacationing with us might sit in on the meetings. Turned out they didn't and were happy fishing while the minutes were being read. The family meeting format establishes a sense of connection and intimacy that is reassuring. It also offers a time of sharing the power and control that all members, particularly the children, relish.

Hurrahs/Boos

During the week nice things can happen that are either only shared by a few, ignored or not celebrated. The "Hurrahs and Boos" portion of the meeting gives time for that. The "Boos" for us designated experiences that brought tears. The name must have originated from "boohoo." Certainly other more eloquent terms could be used. Maybe this part of the agenda could be the "Hurrahs and Dismays?" I recall my husband sharing that he had gotten a raise, and everyone cheered. Getting a good mark on a spelling test, completing a book report, playing tennis with honest players, shoveling the snow off the driveway or playing well in a concert are all worthy moments to share.

Boos can be an opportunity to share tough moments. "I wish I had been selected for the chess team." "I am so sad that my friend has moved to Detroit." I remember Elizabeth being so sad that her sister was off to junior high and she had to stay in elementary school. This is a designated time when family members can say nice things to one another. This time teaches the importance of sharing feelings and not just assuming everyone understands. This is a time when honest and direct conversation eases the pain and shares the joy.

Jokes

Our joke time was not as consistent as the other parts of the agenda. It existed when the children were at a certain age when "knock-knock" jokes and silly humor filled their days. I realize now that our children have grown, they do have a very active joke agenda; however, now they are shared on emails.

Adjournment

Only after the next meeting was planned, could we adjourn. This was difficult on occasion. Sometimes the treats and eats ran out too soon. One time Elizabeth was the chairperson and was fed up with the whole ordeal. She stomped upstairs and retreated to her bedroom. Her father went up to her room and reminded her that we were having a family meeting and she was the chairperson. As chairperson, she could not leave until the agenda was completed. She stomped back downstairs and completed her job.

Family meeting agendas teach "finish what you begin," "hang in there," and commitment. To encourage the meetings we needed to be sure all topics were discussed. Family members were urged to stand up for their ideas. I remember when the topic of cable television was brought up. I said there was no way this family would have cable. My husband stated quite clearly that this family was not run by a dictator and that we would research the question and develop a matrix of needs and wants. Everyone had a job and at a later meeting we all made the decision that cable was not necessary after we completed a matrix focused on needs and wants.

A foreign exchange student lived with us for a few months. She, too, had to sit in on the meetings and share her ideas. Having another person in the house added new agenda items. She became part of the family chores and certainly the family celebrations. Talking about her feelings was new to her. We were interested in her needs and wants. As a visiting member of our family she had the right and responsibility to be clear and included. This was new to her. Actually, sharing her thoughts and feelings was probably stranger to her than learning the ins and outs of American classrooms. She learned quickly, however.

It is important to follow through with action plans and review the outcomes. Children learn about commitment and change. As a result of family meetings, I learned not to shout. I remember sharing at a meeting that I had gone all week without yelling, and no one had noticed. I still smile when I recall the surprise in my daughters' eyes. I hadn't yelled all week and they had failed to cheer. They certainly were quick to notice when I did yell.

I also believe my nagging went down when the white message board went up in the kitchen and completed tasks were erased. The white board was a solution that emerged from a lengthy conversation during a family meeting. The white board became a communication tool. Messages included rides that were needed, laundry that was to be folded and dogs that wanted to be walked. Each day anyone could write his or her needs on the white board. Elizabeth and Heather now have boards hanging in their own kitchens and they appear to be well-used.

Family meetings can be derailed if they are only held during times of crisis. If they are not consistent, predictable and orderly, they will be ignored and quickly become extinct.

Our dedication to family meetings taught us all how to grow and live together in a caring, purposeful way. Family meetings were ways we scheduled time to talk with one another about our lives, problems, concerns and celebrations. We learned how to use "I" messages and were honest in our discussions. "I" messages happen when the person speaking takes responsibility for his or her own statements. Instead of using "you" to begin a comment, "I" is the opening word. Using "I" messages is a way to eliminate blaming or judging statements. It is interesting how beginning a comment with "I" leads to conversation. Beginning with "you" sets the groundwork for a defensive retort. Family meetings teach that your opinion matters. As I look back on our early years, I see mistakes and misjudgments. However, I never will regret a moment of family meetings in which we took ourselves seriously. I believe we take ourselves seriously today because, years ago, we learned how to agree, disagree, problem solve, and to manage money, time and different agendas. We also learned years ago that every family member had something worthwhile to say and the right to be heard.

Family Meeting Possible Topics

The day-to-day life of the family will provide ample ideas for discussion. High functioning companies have regular staff meetings in which all participate and are heard. A family meeting sets a tone of connection, communication and a valuing of each family member. Family work needs to be as important as family celebrations. These are a few suggestions to help parents focus on their own lives and family meeting structure.

Parent participation only

Birth-2 years Sharing responsibility for child care, home care, grocery shopping, couple time and alone time for adults

Parent - child participation

2 - 6 years Toys put away
Family routines including chores, playtime, worktime,bedtime, mealtime
Allowance
Television use

6 - 16 years Friendships
Homework
After-school activities
Family expectations for holidays
Acceptable language in the home
Pet responsibilities
Parent support and behavior at after-school events
Extra curricular activities for all, together and separately
Housework and yard work

Family needs and wants
Individual members needs and wants
Library use
Alcohol, drugs, chemical use
Computer use and Internet access
Movie ratings and selection process
Sibling relationships

16+ years Car use, maintenance and finances
Time management
School work management
Part-time jobs
Sibling relationships
Relationships with other teenagers
Spring break
Family time vs. friend time

Each family needs to find their own topics for conversations

Reflection:

Three Tough Lessons

According to some, the three toughest lessons we must teach our children are about how to get along with others, how to manage their time and how to spend their money.

The relationships children have with family members will often be recreated with their peers. Making a habit of discussing relationships has long-term benefit. Talk with children, listen to children – these are habits that can become lifelong skills. Start when children are young.

Relationships depicted on television provide wonderful opportunities for critical discussion. Grab the opportunity. Don't wait until children are teenagers when discussions may appear suspicious or distrustful. Important in all discussions, no matter what the child's age, is to be respectful of feelings expressed, even when they are different from your own. A parent always needs to be clear about the Red Zone non-negotiables; however, a child does not have to like them. Liking and adhering to them are different.

Time management is a skill that is learned and relearned. Begin teaching at home by modeling good time management skills. Set aside time for weekly and daily planning together. A white board in the kitchen can be a helpful tool for recording daily things to do. Listing tasks provides an opportunity for all to participate in family work. Erasing the board when tasks are done offers time for celebration. Talk about keeping commitments and promises. Be sure as parents you keep yours. Too often children don't have to make decisions and follow through. Decision are made for them. Adults in children's lives need to slow down and allow children to learn to manage time.

Managing money can best be learned by managing money. Start children early with a nominal allowance. Having allowance and chores be contingent on each other isn't recommended. The allowance amount should be small enough to force children to make choices, but large enough for them to save and spend a little. Explain how you as a parent make decisions about money. Let children learn from their mistakes. They will learn early about bargain shopping and looking for quality.

Learning how to get along with others, how to manage time and how to manage money are difficult lessons. Children can and will learn if they are given the opportunity.

Ada

Chapter 16

Red • Yellow • Green Zones: Opportunities for Extension

"Caring is the greatest thing, caring matters most."

Freiderich Von Hugel

Children interact with many adults during many different situations. The Red • Yellow • Green concept can be applied to other interactions. It is not limited to the parent-child relationship. The ideas are simple and can be easily translated so that counselors, childcare providers, grand-parents, juvenile probation officers, foster parents, and classroom teachers, to name but a few, would find the framework application helpful. In presenting the concept to numerous groups, adults from a variety of professions responded comfortably to applying the Red • Yellow • Green idea in their daily work lives. The Red Zone was about limits, boundaries, what is socially not acceptable, and simply "the things we don't do." The Yellow Zone included trust, the child's decisions, responsibilities, privi-leges, choices, areas to start independence, developing competency and "things the child is trusted to do." The Green Zone was described as the area of positive affirma-tions, behaviors liked and appreciated, that which was welcomed and allowed, and "things we always do." The idea is as simple as gym socks. Everyone can understand and use it.

The figure on page 72 illustrates the Red • Yellow • Green Framework over time. The connecting ovals depict the dynamic relationship between the three zones during a specific time. The size of the zones is different for a two-year-old. The Yellow Zone is confined even though the two-year-old thinks he or she can use the mower. Adults need to pay close attention during the child's early application of the Yellow Zone. The Red • Green area for adolescents, although present, should be well instilled within the child. The adolescent has experienced the family rules and routines for years, tested them in other environments and has a clear knowledge of what values the family embraces. The younger child is just learning the differences. The relationship between all three zones is based on the growing and changing needs and aspirations of the child who is present in the Yellow Zone. Family values, rituals and routines are practiced and modeled in the Red and Green Zones and are constants that provide a sense of emotional security.

Many times adults other than parents interact with children and family members. Equipping key adults to use a like language when interacting with the child could be a time-saving and behavior teaching strategy. Developing a consistency of message from childcare providers and nannies would clarify some problem areas. Children are learning all of the time. How helpful to have other adults interacting with the child using the same words. It's wise to take time to be sure all adults interacting with the child agree to manage the Red and Green Zones in a like manner. Just think of the confusing statements that could be eliminated.

I have worked with nannies who worry about the lack of relationship between parents and their children. The message too often is "let the nanny do it." This attitude undermines developing the needed relationship between parents and their children. Talking about this concern using the Red • Yellow • Green Framework could be helpful, friendly and life-saving for the children. It could also be job saving for the nanny. A conversation about what the nanny and the parent see as acceptable Yellow Zone behaviors would minimize confusion between adults and the child. Agreeing on the Reds and Greens will clarify roles, expectations and responsibilities. What I am suggesting is as simple as being sure that everyone knows the rules. How do we come and go? What am I supposed to do? What can I count on you to do? What will we all learn from and with one another? This isn't as simple as it sounds. However, from a Red • Yellow • Green Zone conversation, the answers will emerge.

I have heard from childcare providers that parents have no routine, no schedule at home. Having a conversation about the importance of a Red • Green way things are done in the home would help all of the adults involved. Surely a well-run childcare or a high functioning preschool is built on structure and routine. Good programming for young children requires clear Red and Green expectations. Just by talking about the Reds and Greens, the adults who care for and about the child could establish a shared sense of expectation. Consistent messages and predictable responses are always listed in the child growth and development books as helpful for young children. No hitting at school can transfer easily to no hitting at home. Appreciation of toys being returned to shelves can be reinforced at home. I have watched one-year-olds eagerly throw used napkins in the trash at school. Throwing trash in wastebaskets is as easily accomplished. Trash is thrown, toys put away and no one is hit. Seems to me everyone in the child's life, including the child, thrives.

Adults could have the following conversation: "I am worried about the lack of routines in the home. Let's write up some Red • Green Zones expectations. I think it would be helpful for all of us to understand this." Such a conversation would assure better behavior expectations for the child in different environments. It is better to say, "Mary is nine years old. She is old enough to have her own alarm clock and monitor when her library books need to be returned. Let's talk about the Yellow Zone." That is a much more friendly discussion than saying, "Good grief! Let her grow up. We are raising a child unable to make her own decisions."

Elementary school teachers often talk about parents doing too much for their child. Librarians have watched parents completing their child's science project. Librarians and teachers know that the child should be the student. Teachers know that parents doing the school work gets in the way of the child's learning success. Teachers can have a conversation with parents about the Yellow Zone and help the parent understand their role is to encourage, support and reassure, but not to undermine the opportunity for the child to develop self-competency skills. Parents want their child to succeed. These discussions between the involved adults will recognize that the child needs to be the learner.

Professionals in special education know full well the challenge of sharing pertinent information with parents who have a child who is not typical. Parents of all children need to learn how to parent the child they have instead of trying to parent the child for which they had hoped. This is particularly true with parents of children with special needs. Figuring out how zones might interact by using the color words somehow feels less intrusive and less judgmental. Professionals can gently talk about how Reds and Greens will work and what possible Yellow opportunities might be considered. My experience has been that parents of a special needs child too often do too much for their child. A conversation about the Yellow Zone could help one balance the natural desire to protect.

Competence cannot be parentally or externally determined. A genuine sense of competence comes from within the individual.

A friend's daughter has Down syndrome. After learning the Red • Yellow • Green Framework, my friend found her interactions with her adolescent daughter were eased after she clarified, "This is a Red Zone." The daughter was always happy when the mother said, "This is a Yellow Zone, Sue. This is your choice." All family members learned the language and found the communication between parents and the young girl improved and family relationships strengthened. Everyone liked knowing how, together and separately, they could be a positive influence. As the daughter aged, discussion of self-care, meal preparation, job selection and work responsibility could be topics for family discussion using the Zones as a comfortable base for everyone.

I trained 45 Head Start staff using the Red • Yellow • Green Framework. They found it useful both in the classroom and while making home visits. Talking with families as a home visitor is challenging. Intervention strategies of any sort promote anxiety and a sense of defensiveness in parents. The Head Start staff were working on goal setting and appreciated using simple colors to clarify expectations. Suggestions framed in the Red • Green framework were easy to understand and quickly applied. Parents liked that. Social workers and school psychologists have also found the application useful.

When professionals speak to parents without jargon, a rapport can replace discomfort. Adults working together create an opportunity for student achievement.

Often in parenting classes, frazzled parents have spoken about the challenges of grandparents. Grandparents may buy too much candy or purchase too much stuff. Muddy rules have fractured relationships. How much easier for longed-for connections to have a conversation sharing that "These are the Red and Green expectations of our home." "At our house we eat at the table." "At our house we go to bed at 7:30." "There is no hitting at our house." Grandparents really want to be included in their grandchildren's lives. However, they often need guidance. Sometimes grandparents unknowingly meddle in discipline strategies causing confusion. How much easier it would be to say to doting grandparents, "These are the Red and Green Zones of our home. These are the behaviors we expect and reinforce and the stuff we don't allow. Please expect the same behaviors when you care for

Mark." Such a conversation is necessary and can be held in a friendly manner. Saying, "Unless you follow our rules, you won't see your grandchild" can be harmful to and for everyone. Sharing conversations also could be an opportunity for grandparents to ask, "When would you like my thoughts on child raising?" "I'd like to take Jack fishing. Isn't it time for that in his Yellow Zone?" Clear messages about hitting, biting and the meal process all easily fit into a Red • Yellow • Green Zone discussion.

Discussions like this should also be shared with others who care for children so they can learn to follow parental guidance. Recently, a young mother said, "Throwing things is not OK. Throwing stuff other than a ball is in the Red Zone. Throwing a ball is in the Green Zone. This is what is allowed. This is what isn't." Everyone understood her message, including her two-year-old. The grandmother was able to maintain the object-throwing lesson in her home. Without that discussion, the child might have learned "At my house I can't throw things. But at other people's houses, I can throw whatever I want." What the child learned was the adults in his life agreed about ball throwing.

I remember when my father needed gentle suggestions as to what Heather could be expected to do. Eventually he understood – after I got angry. I reminded him I was the mother and my relationship with Heather was foremost. How I wish I had known the Red • Yellow • Green ideas. We could have talked calmly. Heather would not have witnessed her mother arguing loudly with her grandfather. There is a better way. I only learned it too late.

This framework is not a cookbook of suggestions about what to do. It is a way to think about the parenting practices from the perspective of core values such as trust, care and respect. The framework is designed to help individuals find their own parenting strategies. Those developing materials to help parents can use the Red • Yellow • Green language to help parents sort through piles of suggestions. Thinking about these suggestions simply helps parents act consistently. So many times adults have said to me, "I can do this." That is exactly what a child needs: a parent who believes he or she can be successful. Successful parenting leads to successful children.

Somehow thinking about the Red and Green Zones in your home is less guilt promoting. Parents are tough on themselves. They need a clear but gentle way to think about this difficult role of being their child's teacher. Parents sometimes have way too much outside information. This can eat away at the common sense present in most adults. The Red • Green idea, in its simplicity, can fuel a parent to figure out how to handle a situation without quaking in a corner confused, exhausted and bewildered. Thinking simply can help the parent have courage, promote confidence and consider options thoughtfully. I, for one, don't think well when I am distraught. I become upset when my short-term actions don't match my long-term plans. I can, however, stop and catch my breath and think "Red?" "Yellow?" Such simple thoughts allow for immediate focus and usually a better response. I might add, I have found this concept helpful with my husband, co-workers, and neighbors, one of whom had a snarling dog.

Children come with personal antennae. You can't make your child feel competent, accomplished or self-reliant. They know when they are performing well. Even little ones can say, "I did it." Being told you are terrific and capable doesn't matter if the internal message is one of "I am unable," "I can't," "I am too afraid to try." You can only be responsible for yourself and the way you interact with your child. Providing a safe place for the child to practice skills and experience consequences is something the parent can do. Helping the adults who interact with that child so that messages are consistent adds to a sense of emotional safety. The child, however, is the one on his or her own journey. Parents and other caring adults can watch, cheer and encourage, but the traveler is the child.

Giving children choices and having them make mistakes is both time and energy consuming. Parents and other involved adults making choices takes less time but the lessons are lost.

The Red • Yellow • Green Framework was crafted over the years. Not only did my husband and I have trouble defining our roles together and separately, grandparents, although well meaning, got in the way. Neighbors, friends and even people in the grocery store selecting lettuce all had suggestions. Side or even direct comments from others can confuse parents. We tried to define the Reds and Greens that established the non-negotiables and celebrations in our household. We crafted the "Alden Way." It was our way. It was not the neighbors', my parents' or Dr. Spock's method. I wanted to raise two daughters gently, assure them that they would always matter, and help them learn that certain behaviors were necessary, expected and appropriate. I also wanted them to learn that some behaviors were inappropriate, out-of-line and unacceptable. My husband and I had to come up with something we both understood and could implement. We paid close attention to the Yellow Zones that each of our daughters did differently. Heather and Elizabeth taught us what they needed, how and when to respond so that they, too, would eventually be able to stand strong, capable, self-reliant and competent.

The Red • Yellow • Green Framework is a way of thinking which paves the way for parents to discuss issues that relate to being consistent and present in their children's lives. The colors can trigger a response during moments of confusion or anger. "Is this a Red Zone?" "In our house there is no hitting." "Our children do not have access to the television in their bedrooms." "What is the long term outcome of this action?" The framework also reminds adults to hug and reassure each child, giving important messages from the heart. "Am I noticing my child when he or she is behaving well?" "Do my children only get noticed when they are misbehaving?" "Am I looking for Green Zone behaviors and saying something?" "Do the other adults in my child's life know that this is a Red Zone in our family?" Using the framework is a way of talking about the tough stuff without having to get nasty.

Good parenting requires time for self-reflection and problem-solving consideration. It is helpful for a parent to ask for example, "What are some Green Zone expectations?" "We always brush our teeth before bedtime." A bedtime Yellow Zone would be which pajamas the child wears to bed. I know of a parent who was irate because her child wanted to wear a baseball cap to bed. For her, the cap was a Red Zone. This is probably worth reconsidering. Going to bed is the key issue here. If the child feels wearing a baseball cap helps, so what? What really matters is going to bed, reading a story and turning out the lights. A discussion about the Reds in a home feels less judgmental than saying, "You are letting the children run the household." "What are some ways we might work together to provide clear expectations for the children?" "What is it we want from them at bedtime?" "What do we want to teach them about eating dinner together?" "I have noticed our daughter does not take care of her teeth, brush her hair or take a bath regularly. What are we going to do to help her learn selfcare skills?" Asking questions such as, "Have you found your child in the Green Zone today?" "Have you spent all of your energy saying 'no' and focusing on the Red Zone?" helps evaluate parenting patterns.

Adults need to have conversations about expectations, family routines and how they want to be as a family. Family living requires thoughtful strategies and intentional actions if family connections and communication are to be learned and practiced. Those working with families can use the framework to communicate and teach. As a parent educator, I have been told many times, "There is so much I've applied from this Red • Yellow • Green Framework. The application has not just been as a family member but at my work site." It really is like a gym sock. It can travel anywhere.

Years are spent learning to swim, ice skate and compute numbers. Why do we believe relating with family members and other adults should be quick and easy?

ℛeflection:

Becoming an At-Home Personal Trainer

Star Tribune, March 13, 2002, "Personal coaching for muddled teens?"

Parents who are worried about struggling teens can hire a personal coach to ease the adolescent journey. This, I am sure, is a new and burgeoning job opportunity. Although the qualifications are unclear, I imagine some are at their wits' end, and such a hireling could appear to be an answer.

I am skeptical, however. I don't know that a personal trainer can help a struggling adolescent who is in need of inner assurance, inner self-direction and inner acceptance. I do know that such strengths emerge when a parent is personally a part of a child's growing up.

I watched a father walk his child into the Family Center this morning. They were holding hands as they gingerly crossed the icy tundra of our parking lot. I think, if asked, he would have said he was his daughter's personal trainer and coach.

When Elizabeth was young, she heard about a young girl who received $1,000 to buy clothes for school. The mother had encouraged her to bring back a few hundred dollars. Elizabeth was thrilled. I told her to forget it. She had me. Together we would figure out the maze of school shopping.

Through the years, I kept showing up. I needed to know how she came and went from school events. I attended all of the school conferences with her. She didn't like that much. I told her I had to go as it was in my parent job description. I needed to meet the young men picking her up on a Friday night. I needed to have her attend family events. I needed both children to attend family meetings and participate in our family work. They hoped I would tire of this. I did. My children got in the way of my life. I, however, kept showing up. Truth was, they were teaching me about life.

Parents need to be there for their children from the beginning. Parents are at-home teachers, coaches and personal trainers. Parents need to help children learn how to follow instructions, deal with frustration, trial and error.

Home, according to Harriet Beecher Stowe, is the back room, the learning rehearsal place for much of life's front stage events. Home is where winning and losing are practiced. Home is where lessons about "I love you no matter what" and care, persistence and loyalty are modeled. At the table in the home, teaching "thank you" and "please" is what a parent personal trainer does. In the home, cleaning up rooms, finishing homework and enjoying birthday parties are a part of family living. The home is the workout room, the training center for the rest of your life.

Good parent coaches talk about clear expectations, and assure routines are part of everyday. Good parent coaches encourage their children in the face of both success and failure. An available parent when a child is growing up establishes a positive climate where children feel warmth, acceptance and support.

A top-notch elementary teacher I know believes the most important piece of furniture in the home should be a round wooden table with enough chairs for every family member to sit. This is the table where discussions about the tough stuff occur. This is the table where prayers, "I love you" and "I am scared" can be shared. The more time spent around such a table, the less time would be needed searching the yellow pages trying to find a personal coach for a muddled teenager.

Children who sit at tables with caring adults believe they are not alone. A personal trainer arrived the day they were born and signed up for the long haul. Now, that should be every child's birthright. No outsider need apply.

Ada

Chapter 17

Conclusion

"For every family and for every family member, it is crucial that each person's place is fully recognized, accepted, and understood."

Virginia Satir - Peoplemaking

"Happiness is in the journey, not at the end of the road."

Quilter's saying

These are some of my life lessons. I believe that others may find comfort by thinking through daily decisions using this simple model. I believe those who care for and about children could easily adapt the skills to their work lives. Home daycare providers and early childhood teachers are parent educators as well. Encouraging parents to be responsible and friendly adults can be easily addressed by holding a conversation about Red and Green Zones. Head Start teachers could talk to parents about the emotional security needs of children. Social workers can bring families and teachers together, encouraging family meetings be held in the home and showing how home support of learning needs to happen at the kitchen table. Probation officers have found the Red • Yellow • Green Framework helpful when talking to other adults who are trying to provide care for struggling, seemingly disconnected children.

These shared ideas can have long-lasting impact if carefully applied and persistently woven into the every day fabric of family by purposeful parents. I watch our Elizabeth gently raise her sons. Someone once said, "Be careful how you raise your children; they will parent your grandchildren." As I watch Elizabeth and her husband Jon, I know our grandsons Jack and Charlie Flynn are blessed. Their parents are involved, purposeful and dedicated.

Although our daughters are grown, they come with their husbands and children regularly to Sunday dinners. We now sit around the dinner table and have involved conversations about the world in which we live. I think the implementation of the Red • Yellow • Green Framework early on empowered all of us to think, act and live responsively with and to one another. Authentic relationships emerged from all of those family meetings. Weekly we get together to share the fabric of our lives. Dinner together is not a command performance. The in-depth conversations are a welcomed dessert to our early apprentice years.

David and I have been married for 38 years. Together we have laughed, cried, agonized and delighted. We continue to learn and adjust to our every day. Together we have had the courage to allow each other to find our own way as individuals, and dedicated time and energy necessary to craft a parent hat that emerged from the Red • Yellow • Green Framework.

This book is not a four-course meal. It is, however, a fine bowl of hearty soup with a thick slice of homemade bread. It is simple, filling and will stick to your ribs. I believe it will help build root systems that can sustain families through the years. The framework helps parents think about creating a parenting job description that will last a lifetime. It continues to sustain all of my family. I hope it encourages you, the reader, to find "your way."

Safe Journey.

Reflection:

A Hallway Full of Shoes

It has been a grand holiday. I enjoy the opportunity to revisit my job description as a family member. I also try to pay attention to new bits of information that will help me anchor my thoughts and wits during the wintry days that follow the holiday festivities. I need something to ponder as I shovel, hang on to the wheel on slippery roads, or clutch hot cups of tea trying to warm my hands.

When the children were small, I liked the quiet when they were in bed asleep. Teeth had been brushed, stories read, kisses and hugs shared for all, and a good night said. During the college years, whenever there were four wet toothbrushes in the house, I was thankful. Everyone was home from somewhere.

This holiday, again, they came home. So, however, did their friends. Our hallway was a most amazing array of shoes for two weeks. Our home is modest. However, we had room for people to sleep, laugh, eat and "hang out." Everyone chopped wood, stirred pots of fancy stew, played games, pushed grocery carts, folded towels and sat at the dinner table for hours.

Early in the morning, when everyone was asleep everywhere, I would go down and just look at the shoes in the hall. Somehow we did something right. For some reason, they came with their friends, happy to share their stories.

I really did figure out from all of this that a family member's job just might be to be a cheerleader. It is not up to anyone of us to tell someone else how to live his or her life. When we can be there for one another, be reassuring, comment on how doing your best is good enough, let others know that someone thinks personally they have value and will be in their corner—that may be the greatest gift of all. To tell someone to keep on keeping on may be enough.

I am learning everyday. I now know that a hallway full of shoes is one of the finest decors.

Ada

Sources

Angelou, Maya.
 I Know Why the Caged Bird Sings.
 Random House. Inc. 2002
Briggs, Dorothy.
 Your Child's Self Esteem.
 Doubleday & Company, Inc. 1975
Clarke, J., Dawson, C., and Bredehoft, D.
 How Much is Enough?
 Marlowe & Company. 2004
Coloroso, Barbara.
 Kids Are Worth It! Giving Your Child the Gift of Inner Discipline
 Avon Books New York 1994
Doherty, William J. Ph.D.
 The Intentional Family.
 Addison-Wesley Publishing Company, Inc. 1997
Feste, Catherine.
 The Physician Within
 Henry Holt and Company. 1993
Gossen, Diane Chelsom.
 Restitution: Restructuring School Discipline
 New View Publications. 1992
Kurcinka, Mary Sheedy
 Raising Your Spirited Child
 HarperCollins Publishers. 1991
Reardon, Ruth
 Listening to the Littlest
 C.R. Gibson Co. 1984

Satir, Virginia
 Peoplemaking
 Science and Behavior Books, Inc. 1972
 Avanta - The Virginia Satir Network
 www.avanta.net
Swift, Madelyn
 Discipline for Life: Getting it Right with Children
 Stairway Education Programs 1995
Wheatley, Margaret J.
 Turning to One Another
 Berrett-Koehler Publishers, Inc. 2002

I have made a sincere attempt to obtain permission to quote others, copyrighted material. A few with whom I have been unable to connect are included. I continue to try to connect with these authors or their publishers.

Books can be purchased through Oleanna Books
 P.O. Box 141020
 Minneapolis, Minnesota 55414
 Oleannabks@aol.com
 612-722-5861

Selected Readings

Agassi, Ph.D. Martine. *Hands Are Not for Hitting.*
Free Spirit Publishing. 2000

Bateson, Mary Catherine. *Composing A Life.* A Plume Book. 1990

Carson, Rachel. *The Sense of Wonder.* The Nature Company. 1990

Davis, Laura & Keyser, Janis. *Becoming The Parent You Want To Be.*
Broadway Books. 1997

Edelman, Marian Wright. *The Measure of Our Success.* Beacon Press.
1992

Grollman, Earl A., & Sweder, Gerri L. *The Working Parent Dilemma.*
Beacon Press. 1986

Hanh, Thich Nhat. *The Miracle of Mindfulness.* Beacon Press. 1987

Garbarino Ph.D., James. *Raising Children in a Socially Toxic
Environment.* Jossey-Bass Publishers. 1995

Kaufman, G., & Raphael, Lev. *The Dynamics of Power: Building
A Competent Self.* Schenkman Publishing Company. 1983

Kotulak, Ronald. *Inside the Brain.* Andrews McMeel Publishing.
1997

Lindbergh, Anne Morrow. *Gift From The Sea.* Vintage Books. 1991

Louv, Richard. *Childhood's Future.* Houghton Mifflin Company.
1990

May, Rollo. *Power and Innocence. A Search for the Sources of Violence.*
W. W. Norton & Company. 1972

Morse, Robin K., & Wiley, Meredith S. *Ghosts from the Nursery:*
The Atlantic Monthly Press. 1997

National Research Council Institute of Medicine. *From Neurons to
Neighborhood.* National Academy Press. 2000

Pipher, Ph.D., Mary. *The Shelter of Each Other.* G.P. Putnam's Sons.
1996

Philadelphia Child Guidance Center. *Your Child's Emotional Health.*
Macmillan Publishing Company. 1993

Straus, Murray A. *Beating The Devil Out of Them.* Lexington Books.
1994

Notes

Notes

Notes

About the Author

Ada Alden has been working with parents for nearly 30 years and holds advanced degrees in education and behavior analysis. Ada holds a doctorate from The University of Minnesota and is a nationally certified family life educator. She consults with school districts, working with teachers on parent involvement and effective teacher-parent relationships. Ada has provided training for Head Start staff, child care providers, parents and staff from both the corporate and medical fields. She is the director of family educational services for the Eden Prairie Schools and an adjunct professor at the University of Minnesota and St. Cloud University. She reviews parenting books and writes columns for local newsletters and newspapers.

Ada can be reached through
cranepublishers@aol.com
763-557-2922 • Fax: 763-557-2922